natalie lue

the joy of saying no

A SIMPLE PLAN TO STOP PEOPLE PLEASING, RECLAIM BOUNDARIES, AND SAY YES TO THE LIFE YOU WANT

HARPER HORIZON

For Emmon, Saria, and Nia.

Every day, you remind me of the joy

and the gift of saying no.

Published by Harper Horizon, an imprint of HarperCollins Focus LLC.

Book design by Neuwirth & Associates, Inc.

Any internet addresses, phone numbers, or company or product information printed in this book are offered as a resource and are not intended in any way to be or to imply an endorsement by Harper Horizon, nor does Harper Horizon vouch for the existence, content, or services of these sites, phone numbers, companies, or products beyond the life of this book.

ISBN 978-0-7852-9045-2 (eBook)
ISBN 978-0-7852-9044-5 (HC)
ISBN 9781400335480 (ANZ)
ISBN 9781400335497 (UK)
ISBN 9781400337323 (India)

Library of Congress Control Number: 2022934018

Printed in the United States of America
22 23 24 25 26 LSC 10 9 8 7 6 5 4 3 2 1

CONTENTS

INTRODUCTION

Find Your Joy, Find Your No

'm Natalie Lue, and I'm a recovering people pleaser. Suppressing and repressing my needs, desires, expectations, feelings, and opinions to try to influence and control other people's feelings and behavior was as natural to me as breathing. I thought it was normal to tell people what they want to hear (read: lie) to make them feel better. I believed I was ticking the boxes of being a Good Person by being kind, generous, hard-working, conscientious, loving, eager to help, attractive, and intelligent, and doing what others needed and wanted. It baffled me though that, well, I felt like shit most of the time. It didn't make sense to me that I devoted so much time, energy, effort, and emotion to trying to do the right thing—being a Good Girl—making sure others were pleased and sacrificing myself, yet I did not feel good.

I saved *no* for 911 occasions where my back was against the wall, expressed it in an over-apologetic fashion that suggested I was doing wrong, or said it belatedly in an eruption of pent-up anger and frustration. I thought that saying no because you wanted to, whether it was out of necessity, desire, or even obligation, was something other people did—you know, the ones who'd earned that right with their worthiness. This meant that I typically signed, sealed, and delivered a *no* with pain, anxiety, guilt, resentment, and shame.

* * *

ONE MORNING IN early August 2005, I discovered that *I could say no simply because I wanted to*. On that particular day, I sat in a consultant's office in the lung clinic of a North London hospital braced for the bad news I knew was coming. For eighteen months, I'd traipsed in and out of various departments, sometimes weekly, for chest X-rays, lung function tests, blood tests, CT scans, and general poking and prodding after being diagnosed with a mystery immune system disease (sarcoidosis) that had nearly left me blind in one eye and made me an expert at hiding severe joint pain. A few weeks earlier while on holiday in Egypt celebrating finishing a year's course of aggressive steroid treatment, I'd found a lump in my neck that signaled the disease was "back." Now I knew what it felt like to be Jamie Lee Curtis's character in the *Halloween* films thinking that Michael Myers was gone only for him to reappear to destroy everyone's lives, again.

"... the steroid treatment hasn't worked ... As you know, we don't know what causes it, and there is no cure, so you will need to take steroids for life ... Crucial that you start straight away ... avoid pulmonary heart failure by the age of forty ... no other options ... preserving mobility ..."

I'd recently turned twenty-eight, and as my consultant's voice slipped into a monotone, it hit me: I'd been sick for at least two years, and while I'd understood that my illness was serious, I'd done whatever doctors told me, and my focus had been being at everyone else's service even when I didn't want to be.

Instances of compliance and self-neglect flashed through my mind. I'd decided not to "burden" my family with "too much" information about my illness because I knew they couldn't handle it (and admittedly, their attitudes—including being more concerned about how much weight I'd put on with the steroids—stressed me out). My boss and colleagues were in the dark about the extent of my illness because I'd decided to act as if I weren't ill and to compensate for any "inconveniences," such as appointments and putting steroids in my eye every hour, with high performance.

I'd start the day screaming in agony, and by the time I got off the Tube and entered the office, I had a veneer of calm.

That's why when I heard *no* moments later—resonant, unapologetic, and decided—I looked around to see who had said it. The look of confusion and irritation on my consultant's face made it clear that it had been me.

Normally I'd feel anxious about saying no to an "authority" and appearing "difficult," but this feeling was absent. Fear of dying by age forty far outweighed the potential discomfort I tended to sense in others when I so much as contemplated saying no, never mind verbalizing or showing it. It hit me that no one was coming to save me. It was my responsibility to make decisions and take care of myself.

So I explained that since they didn't know why I had the disease and the steroids clearly weren't solving anything, I was going to explore other options. Cue him reiterating everything he'd already said, pooh-poohing alternatives, and telling me I didn't have any options.

It would have been easy to back down and then spend the next few months or even years stewing over my silencing myself. Instead, I said, "I hear all of that, but I'm still going to explore other options." I promised to attend all of my checkups and that if they weren't seeing any improvement in three months, I'd begin steroid treatment. But that never happened.

Eight months later, I was in remission from my incurable disease, had begun radically overhauling every area of my life, and was in a new relationship with my now husband. Yes, I did employ some alternative therapies (kinesiology and acupuncture), but it was hearing the term *boundaries* not long after that appointment that changed—and saved—my life. Over the seventeen years since that fateful day, time and time again, the solution to almost every struggle and problem has proven to be the same as it was back then: embracing the joy of saying no.

WHEN I SAID no in the consultant's office, I hadn't been in even *one* healthy romantic relationship. Even my dates turned into toxic encounters where, due to rationalizing inappropriate behavior or feeling guilty about my lack of interest, I'd continue to experience violations and/or upgrade the person to "boyfriend." Thanks to my mommy and daddy issues stemming from abandonment, criticism, and chaos, I was in a constant cycle of family drama and was burned-out at work and even in some friendships. I hated myself and my life because it felt like nothing I did was ever enough. Even so, in my mind, *no* led to pain, rejection, failure, disappointment, and abandonment.

I'm not alone. We live in a world that socializes us from early childhood to be people pleasers and to believe that boundaries are wrong and selfish. Yes, we're taught about certain dangers and about how *no* means *no*, but we then receive such confusing and conflicting messages about compliance and how to be loved and safe that many of us lose the ability to say no with confidence. We learn that *no* means *no* as long as it doesn't involve hurting someone or pissing them off or being a "bad" person.

We learn early on that it's critical to please your parents and caregivers in whatever form that takes because, well, they "know best" and we depend on them for survival and love. Work hard at school. Be the best. If you're not the best, be good. Live our dreams, make us proud, don't embarrass us with the neighbors. Be seen and not heard, keep your feelings to yourself. Stop being so sensitive. Work hard and you will get the grades. Be good and you'll receive praise, peace, friendship, and relationships, and avoid undesirable outcomes. Do the things we expect of you. Let that relative hug you even though you're clearly uncomfortable because you will offend them if you don't. Be "nice" so you're not seen as aggressive. Be "good" so people don't think you're slutty and ruin our reputation. Do you see those things we don't like about those other people? Don't do that. When you get the grades, you'll get into university or get a job. From there, you'll get the money, the home, the relationship, and the kids. Basically, be good and you will be a success.

At some point, we discover that the world doesn't work this way. For instance, maybe we do all the right things at work. Yet someone who has no problem making waves and doing all the things we think would be displeasing gets the promotion. We try to be the Perfect Partner, yet they leave us for someone who flies in the face of everything we've been told, or we play the Nice Guy in the hope that the person will see us as relationship material, only to be friend-zoned. We do all the things our parents told us to do and even put our dreams and aspirations on hold, only for them to prefer our sibling, continue guilting us, or never acknowledge anything we do.

And after all this effort, we might realize that we don't know who we are or what we want.

There's no tipping point of people pleasing where we finally win big and all our suffering and effort pay off. Here we are all sacrificed and suppressed up to the hilt, and we're in sucky relationships wondering what's wrong with us, or bored, bullied, underpaid, or burned-out in careers that we were told would lead to our happiness and success. We have no real idea of how to take care of ourselves and meet our needs.

Here's the truth: What I thought was being "good" and "helping out" was people pleasing—using "pleasing" to influence and control other people's feelings and behavior to gain attention, affection, approval, love, and validation or to avoid conflict, criticism, stress, disappointment, loss, rejection, and abandonment.

While some instances of people pleasing are obvious because we know that we're doing something to be liked, allergic to saying no, praise hungry, or maybe behaving like a performing seal on steroids, many of our people-pleasing habits are out of view yet insidious, such as the following:

- Putting off speaking to a coworker about an issue with their work and then staying late or delaying your own work because you worry about hurting their feelings, being bad-mouthed to other team members, or looking incompetent.
- Deciding to eat your mother's chocolate pie even though you have a gluten sensitivity and are lactose intolerant because you'd rather grapple with an upset stomach and being stuck in the bathroom than chance disappointing her or hurting her feelings.

- Calling yourself *too sensitive*, *needy*, *selfish*, and *difficult*, because you feel uncomfortable and increasingly resentful about the friend who repeatedly dumps on you while never taking an interest in what's going on in your life.
- Listening to a date talk about past relationships and difficulties and then deciding that you won't ask for or expect certain things so that they don't feel pressured or in pain, or suddenly feeling invested because you think that you can be the solution to their problems.

Whether overtly or indirectly, you often have an issue with saying no through your words and actions. You do "good" things, but for the wrong reasons.

Think back to some of the times when you haven't said no, whether verbally or through your actions.

Were you being nice, or were you scared?

Were you being nice, or were you angry?

Were you being nice, or were you disappointed?

Were you being giving, loving, and helpful, or were you asking for or expecting something?

Did you really want to do that thing, or were you anxious?

The Joy of Saying No is about how to reclaim yourself from the cycle of people pleasing and supercharge your relationships and experiences by discovering the healing and transformative power of *no*.

Learning to say no didn't just help me recover from that life-threatening illness.

- After my diagnosis, I advocated for my needs at work, gaining full support from human resources and my then boss, including reduced hours while recovering. When they later messed me about with incorrect maternity pay and a botched promotion and return to work, my improved relationship with *no* meant gracefully but assertively drawing my line. This paved the way to writing full-time and starting my business, allowing me to spread healing and joy by sharing the teachings from my transformation on my website, BaggageReclaim .com, with many thousands of people around the world.

- Gradually, I transformed the very codependent, painful relationships I had with my family by allowing myself to step back and redefine my sense of responsibility and obligation. The guilt and anxiety that plagued every interaction has lessened, but there's a little there to remind me to stay in my lane and acknowledge our differences. I finally allowed myself to become a grown-up at twenty-eight, and again and again to the present day, and guess what? The sky hasn't fallen down.

- I cut ties with exes and opted out of shady and unworkable dating situations at much earlier points without second-guessing myself, opening me up to meeting my now husband and being able to grow in the relationship because I endeavored to be myself.

- *No* has helped me be a better mother to myself as well as to my children. Although I still have most of the friends I had before I began my recovery, all the relationships are more balanced and authentic.

- Starting to say no set me on a path of healing trauma, including my fear of abandonment and the pain and anger I carried from abuse. My body's stress responses calmed down, the drama in my life dropped dramatically, and I've learned to navigate challenges when they do arise.

- When my father was diagnosed with bowel cancer in June 2016 after our being estranged for four years, everything I'd learned helped us have a beautiful, forgiving relationship in his final ten months. Afterward, as I wrestled with grief, turning forty, and feeling lost, yet again, *no* came to the rescue, allowing me to experience so much unexpected joy and bringing me to a place where I'm the most me I've ever been.

This is a small sample, and I will share stories from my journey, as well as those of others I've helped along the way, throughout this book. I used to think that I was weird and that my problems and situations were unique, but in August 2005, when I spoke out loud about my struggles on my then personal blog, I was inundated with messages from people saying, "You're me—you're just like me."

You're not alone.

If you don't say yes authentically, you say it resentfully, fearfully, or avoidantly, and that leads to far more problems than if you'd just said no in the first place. It's time to stop living the lie that is people pleasing.

PART 1

GREETINGS, PEOPLE PLEASER

1

ARE YOU A
PEOPLE PLEASER?

DO ANY OF THESE STATEMENTS
SOUND FAMILIAR TO YOU?

- Even though I might disguise, suppress, and repress it, I often feel resentful, obliged, overwhelmed, guilty, anxious, overloaded, drained, exhausted, low, helpless, powerless, or victimized.
- I put other people's needs and wants ahead of my own and feel as if I come last.
- I worry about not being liked, getting into trouble, hurting feelings, looking like a "bad" or "selfish" person, or being rejected, abandoned, or alienated if I say no, express needs, have limits, or am honest.
- I say yes without considering the meaning and consequences and then feel trapped, overwhelmed, anxious, or resentful, or piss people off due to backing out or not having the bandwidth or skill set.
- I struggle to ask for help and fear being a burden and inconveniencing or discomforting others, resulting in routinely dismissing my own needs, expectations, desires, feelings, and opinions as my being oversensitive/needy/difficult/selfish/demanding.

- I say yes based on feeling guilty, afraid, obliged, or anxious.
- I've had stress-related illness or burnout or felt tipped over the edge into a temper that left me feeling ashamed.
- I have little or no time for myself, whether it's for my priorities, enjoyment, or self-care, but I know how to take care of and make time for everyone else.
- I'm the go-to person, whether it's with work, family, friends, or exes that pop back into my life when they're at a loose end.
- I fear that I'm not good enough, and I blame it for other people's feelings and behavior or life not going my way.
- My interpersonal relationships tend to involve my trying to rescue, fix, or change others or my being their pet project.
- I've missed out on things I genuinely want to do because I've said yes to something I shouldn't have.
- I've been involved with an emotionally unavailable or abusive person, and I continued dating/hooking up with/getting back together with them or stayed in the relationship despite its being unfulfilling or unhealthy.
- I worry that my success, happiness, or personal growth will outshine others or cause them to feel unhappy, left out, or abandoned.
- When people don't acknowledge, appreciate, and reward my efforts, I feel wounded, resentful, neglected, abandoned, depressed, used, or abused.
- I'm self-critical, fear failure and making mistakes, overperform and overcompensate, or hide out and coast.
- I struggle to say no at work because I'm afraid of looking lazy or incompetent, seeming as though I'm not a good team player or promotion material, or risking burning bridges or inviting retaliation.
- I use hints to try to get others to meet my needs and wants or to understand my feelings rather than communicate these directly.
- Sometimes I'm fuming or panicking in my head when people ask or expect me to do something, yet I still say yes.
- I give too much.

- I say yes, go along with things, or stay silent even when it's to the detriment of my well-being because I'm afraid to say no or don't know how to say no.

If you answered yes to even one of these statements, you are a people pleaser. These are clues from your body, mind, and life that you do what for all intents and purposes might be "good things" but for the *wrong reasons*—and *that's* what makes it people pleasing.

> People pleasing is consciously and unconsciously suppressing and repressing your needs, desires, expectations, feelings, and opinions to put other people first so that you gain attention, affection, approval, love, or validation or avoid conflict, criticism, disappointment, loss, rejection, or abandonment.

There are people doing the same or similar to you, such as helping out, working hard, wanting to do good things, and feeling uncomfortable about inconveniencing or disappointing people, but they don't come from a place of fear, guilt, obligation, or feeling unworthy. They're aware of their motivations, and in situations where their actions and choices or other people's expectations and requests impact their well-being or are straight-up harmful, inappropriate, or unnecessary, they consider themselves. They'll say no if they need to, want to, or should. They have assertive, active responses.

It's not that they don't care about what others think or that they don't share your wants or fears—they do—but they're not driven by people pleasing, and so they have a greater sense of who they are, including what they need, want, expect, feel, and think. As a result, they're more inclined to let their values and boundaries guide them rather than *should*s, rules, and their perceptions of other people's feelings and behavior. In instances where with the benefit of hindsight they realize that something didn't work for them and was problematic or harmful in some way because, you know, they're human, they allow themselves to learn from that.

People pleasing is a collection of passive-response strategies, rooted in childhood, for avoiding pain and feeling worthy, deserving, accepted, and safe that instead result in chronic feelings of low self-worth, anxiety, resentment, and undesirable outcomes. People pleasing holds you back from being more of who you are and enjoying truly intimate and fulfilling relationships because it doesn't allow you to learn your authentic *yes*, *no*, and *maybe*.

Each one of the statements I listed at the beginning of the chapter reflects incidences where you don't say yes consciously or because you truly want or need to but because, on some level, you are afraid or experiencing misplaced and disproportionate guilt, trying to control something, or hoping that you will be rewarded in some way for going along with things. You also do things not because you want to but because it's what you think is expected of you. If this weren't the case, you'd say no when you need, want to, or should, or you'd certainly say it a helluva lot more than you have now and in the past.

The more of these statements you agree with, the more people pleasing permeates your life. But it's also crucial to acknowledge that even if it's "just" one or a few statements, it's the degree to which it or they affect your life and how authentic and mindful you are that matters.

If you'd like more insight into what each of the statements mean, I've created a handy PDF guide that you can download from thejoyofsayingno.com/resources.

It's impossible to avoid saying no or to be fearful of the consequences of boundaries and not be a people pleaser. You'll keep experiencing variations of the same frustrations, hurts, and problems and mistakenly attribute these to failing to please enough.

The *only* reason we don't say no, or we say yes inauthentically, is because of our emotional baggage, the unresolved hurts, losses, judgments, and old misunderstandings that we carry from the past. We can call it being "nice" or being a "good person" or claim we don't want to "hurt feelings" or "get hurt" or whatever, but it's all code for *Something happened in the past, and I did or didn't like how it made me feel or what happened. So I came up with a story and habit that informed how I respond in similar situations or around similar people, as well as who I believe I have to be. And then I've repeated it.*

All humans have emotional baggage, so having it doesn't make any of us weird, wrong, or different. But *how much we carry* and *its effect on us* reflects our willingness to work through emotional hurts and difficulties. People pleasing blocks this work because between the childlike habits of thinking and behavior; the obligation, guilt, and resentment; and the playing roles in our relationships like the Over- or Underachiever, the Peacekeeper, or the Indispensable Overgiving Helper Who Doesn't Have Any Needs of Their Own, we adopt a mask that distances us from ourselves and others. Ironically, our people pleasing reinforces the very emotional hurts and difficulties that we're trying to avoid or resolve.

That means that we can spend our entire lives trying to get people to *see* us, *hear* us, *validate* us, and meet our unmet needs without realizing that our people pleasing is blocking intimacy and preventing people from seeing the real us. It doesn't allow us to truly feel, hence why we struggle to decipher our boundaries and what we need, desire, expect, feel, and think.

We strive to be good and show how good we are, to throw our effort into things, to save others from themselves, to avoid making ourselves or others uncomfortable, and, yes, sometimes to prove how good we are by suffering, all so that we can gain attention, affection, approval, love, and validation. We also need, want, sometimes *crave* genuine intimacy and connection but don't realize that in our quests to please, we're living lies and hiding.

When we wear masks or costumes, people cannot see (or hurt) the real us. That's *why* we're doing it. We may have shape-shifted our way through life trying to be all things to all people so much that we couldn't pick out the real us in a police lineup!

Our people pleasing has blocked us from learning that without running the risk of conflict and criticism by being honest about who we are through our *yes*es and *no*s, there is no intimacy. Instead, we normalize tiptoeing and walking on eggshells around our own and other people's agendas and good intentions and thinking that this is as good as it gets.

You DIDN'T FALL out of the sky and just *decide* to become a people pleaser. Even if you've had an awareness of it only in adulthood, your people pleasing is something that's been with you since childhood. A combination of socialization, conditioning, and self-taught responses and lessons have trained you to use putting others ahead of you as a strategy for meeting your needs and avoiding risk and hurt.

I don't say this to you as if you and I are different and I'm some enlightened human being beyond emotional baggage. I still people-please sometimes because I spent most of my life doing it without even realizing that it *was* people pleasing. I just thought it was How Life Works and What Natalie Should Do.

When I sense the potential for conflict or conflict is actually happening, I still freeze momentarily and want to moonwalk away from the situation or instantly camouflage into the surroundings. I still fret about people's reactions; sometimes want my parents, even my dead father, to be different from who they are; sometimes spend far too long trying to write a short text or email; and can suck the feckin' joy out of pretty much anything if I let my (recovering) perfectionist ways get near it.

People pleasing is code for *I am (or was) anxious about something*. It's an anxiety-management habit that ironically keeps you locked in a cycle of anxiety because it's hypervigilance. When you're effectively on high alert and constantly scanning the perimeter for disapproval or danger, it inhibits your ability to be conscious, aware, and present. And it's being willing to recognize this and how my baggage shows up in that moment that's allowed me to make more mindful, *joyful* choices.

* * *

I'M A RECOVERING people pleaser because, just like you, my adulthood is about unlearning all the unproductive and harmful messages and lessons I've picked up along the way so that I can heal, grow, and learn through letting me become more of my authentic self instead of hiding it.

Instead of being in my own *Groundhog Day* thinking and doing the same people-pleasey things and expecting different results, I've acknowledged that the way I sometimes think, feel, behave, and choose reflects old pain, fear, and guilt, not who I am. I'm allowing myself to recover and flourish from what I've been through by using *no* as a way to heal my emotional baggage as I go through life. You can too. This, incidentally, is far better than people pleasing in an attempt to "work on yourself" to become "baggage-free" and finally worthy enough of being, doing, and having more of what you need, desire, and deserve.

I can't overstate this enough: People pleasing is a misappropriation of your good qualities and bandwidth (time, energy, effort, and emotions), not who you really are. The effects are felt in your life, from how you feel or don't feel inside, to the intimacy of your relationships, to your workload, to what might be secret hurts and resentments, to your general sense of fulfillment and connectedness. Depending on your level of people pleasing, your body might be in near-constant fight-flight-freeze mode, and rather than releasing you, this hypervigilance is compounding whatever you've been through that contributed to why you people-please.

You don't have to wait until you're "enough" or "perfect." You came into the world enough and will leave here enough. It's that you've internalized a lot of shite along the way that's taught and convinced you otherwise. And you don't need to be perfect—aka inhuman and without emotional baggage—you need to declutter, unpack, and tidy up whatever's getting in the way of your saying no *so that you can also* learn to say yes authentically. You need to unlearn being anxious about yourself and displeasing everyone so that you can access a far wider range of emotions and healthily take care of yourself *and* your relationships.

The truth is, we're often trying to gain self-worth and self-esteem as well as get the benefits of more fulfilling interpersonal relationships and experiences by *earning it* with our pleasing so that we don't have to risk vulnerability—and that's not going to cut it if we genuinely want to experience more intimacy, fulfillment, peace, and *joy* in our lives. To decide to choose what to let go of means confronting why we accumulated it in the first place and connecting with our true intentions and values, and that's what I'm here to help you with.

- Knowing how and when to say no is about understanding your boundaries, the visible and invisible lines between you and others that show your awareness of where you end and they begin.

- Your boundaries communicate what you know about who you are and want to be, your responsibilities, and your awareness of who others are and their responsibilities.

- All problems we encounter have a boundary issue in there somewhere, so the more we differentiate between our feelings, thoughts, bodies, and stuff, and someone else's, the better we become at not just solving our problems but also not repeating the same problem.

- The mistake that most humans make is conflating boundaries with saying no, but boundaries are *as much* about what you say yes to. So when you've treated *no* like a dirty word and focused on *yes*, you've indirectly said no to being more you and stuck with the people-pleasing cycle.

- Think of *yes* and *no* like the heart and lungs, which work closely together to pump oxygen-rich blood around the body. It's not a case of using one or the other; when one organ is compromised, it affects not only the other but also how the entire body functions.

- If you're afraid to say no, you also have a problem with other people's *no*s, and it's time to consider what it is that you do, and what you avoid, to lessen their *no*.

- Everything you do is about trying to meet needs: the things you need to be, do, and have not merely to survive but thrive. The healthier your boundaries, the more you'll meet your needs because you're owning and being yourself, so allowing yourself to say no allows you to fill up the void of the unmet needs that you've been (ineffectively) using people pleasing to meet.

- Your boundaries *are* your needs, desires, expectations, feelings, and opinions because these represent who you are and how you want to be, your *values*, preferences, principles, and priorities for living your life happily and authentically. They are your *yes*, *no*, and *maybe*, so in essence, the more you represent who you are by showing up and stepping up authentically and honestly, the healthier your boundaries are. If you're not authentically saying yes and saying no when you need, should, or want to, you become incongruent with your values because you are not embodying your character or honoring your preferences and priorities.

- When you people-please, you're suppressing your boundaries because you are suppressing *yourself*. You are your boundaries.

- How willing you are to honor your boundaries is an expression of your self-esteem, the sum of the thoughts you feed yourself, and the way you treat yourself. When you treat and regard yourself as a worthwhile and valuable person, you have the confidence to be more you. And even if you don't feel so good about yourself yet, creating healthier boundaries paves the way to matching how you feel about yourself with your better treatment of yourself.

2

IN THE BEGINNING

When I ask twenty- to eightysomethings why they don't, for instance, say no at work or to family, or why they go along with things even when they feel wrong, time and again, their answers are often about fear of "getting into trouble" and how they have to "do as they're told." Essentially, they want to be "good." So what's going on here, and how did we learn to be people pleasers?

Assuming you're not a child right now, you were raised during the Age of Obedience. Driven by strictness, discipline, and control, this style of raising, interacting with, and communicating with children centered on making them "good" by teaching them to unconditionally obey authority figures, instilling a sense of obligation, and, ultimately, ensuring they were compliant, excessively prone to agreeing with others. This prepared us for work and being adults that meet society's expectations.

While just like olden times, modern parents and caregivers can be involved, distant, neglectful, or abusive, a stark difference with recent parenting is that there's two-way, instead of one-way, dialogue and respect. Awareness of children's rights, respect of their boundaries, and nurturance of their emotional, mental, and physical well-being are no longer anomalies ascribed to "hippie" or "lax" parenting. It's also more widely understood that children are their own people, not the property of adults, so children have more autonomy.

While humans have always been preoccupied with "being good" and relied on a level of compliance and fitting in as a means of survival and meeting needs, the meaning of "being good" has changed as human civilization has advanced. In fact, if you trace the etymology of the word *good*, you see how it was initially associated with religion and gradually evolved to include success, prosperity, and then work ethic and being "well-behaved." This evolution tracks with what was happening in the world, including the Industrial Revolution, colonization, and imperialism.[1]

During the Age of Obedience, somebody somewhere was policing or dismissing our feelings; labeling our facial expressions, personalities, introversion or extroversion, behavior, appearances, intellects, talents, or aspirations as "good" or "bad" and in effect guilting, obliging, scaring, and shaming us into being whom they wanted us to be. It was socially acceptable to physically "discipline" and punish a child whether in public or private, or to say whatever you wanted without thought for the emotional and mental consequences. Emotional, mental, and physical connections were not a priority or the norm, so the desire for attention, affection, and nurturing were seen as surplus to requirements.

It also wasn't uncommon for children to raise their siblings or to even parent their parents, or to forgo an education to earn a living or be married off to someone the family could benefit from. Parents and caregivers could engage in what we would now regard as unsafe behavior without regard for its impact. When we, as children, experienced bullying, low confidence, depression, academic challenges, racism and prejudice, exploitation, abuse, or neglect, or didn't present in a neurotypical or gender-conforming fashion, there was a lack of support, and the solution to everything was to find a way to be "good." This meant that our struggles often became a question of what we'd failed to be and do—*What were you wearing?* or *What did you say to upset them?*—rather than addressing the actual problem, making the masking of our pain, struggles, and needs a form of obedience and self-protection.

While we all learned shameful messages in childhood that silenced our true selves, gendered messaging around goodness meant very different lessons around assertiveness. This means that girls and then women are more likely to be socialized into a compliance that limits their agency and personal power whereas boys and then men learn compliance to facilitate gaining more power. It's that not-so-subtle difference between *Be meek and mild, be ladylike and don't make waves* and *Do as you're told but also buck up and be a man, not a sissy, so that you can preserve manliness and be a success.*

So although anyone can be a people pleaser, women are more likely to be simply because, thanks to patriarchy, men are less likely to be penalized for asserting themselves in even the most basic of ways, whereas many sections of society still frown upon women doing the same.

By emphasizing compliance, society instilled a sense of fear and guilt but peddled it as respect. This resulted in a fear of not just the potential or actual negative consequences of not complying but the fear of authorities themselves. Authority figures were treated as if they were automatically right and safe, so the presumption was that if we felt otherwise, we were disrespectful.

The Age of Obedience didn't teach nuance; it taught unconditional compliance. Specifically, it taught the criticalness of obeying anybody with authority over you, which in childhood, is anyone whom you perceived to have power over you. This meant that we learned about "stranger danger" in the form of a kidnapper or creepy figure with a bag of candy, but no one explained that thanks to all our obedience training, not only could strangers invoke the same fear, guilt, and compliance as loved ones, but also that often the people we needed danger awareness about were people whom we automatically trusted and revered because of their status and profession, such as priests, teachers, police officers, family friends, and extended family.

We learned that if we didn't obey people in positions of authority, it could not only mean problems for us but for those around us too. It's why abusers tend to dangle the threat of something happening to loved ones or suggest that it would be problematic or inconvenient for them to know about the abuse. And, of course, we complied because we depended on our parents and caregivers for survival.

This language of emotional blackmail activates our consciences so that guilt (and shame) make us likely to acquiesce. Rules (arbitrary or not), along with obligations (false or not) and expectations and requests (realistic, fair, or not) are couched in guilt. After a while, it becomes the voice in our head, and we become adept at emotionally blackmailing ourselves into complying. Much as there might be people in our lives who pressure us, when we take stock of who talks us into saying yes, it's often us scaring and guilting ourselves into doing things. Feeling guilty is so intertwined with our intimate relationships that we sometimes confuse it with love and care.

We experience guilt when we have (or perceive ourselves to have) committed wrongdoing. In a world that teaches you to distrust your feelings and to think that your needs, desires, and expectations are selfish and shameful, you wind up with a disproportionate sense of wrongdoing that translates into *Let me spend my life compensating for or preempting badness by being a people pleaser.*

The Age of Obedience taught us to go against ourselves whenever we perceive a rule, obligation, threat, or potential reward. It's why work environments can be so triggering. The combination of authorities and fear of disobeying plunges us right back into childlike feelings, thoughts, and behavior.

I work with clients who are deeply perplexed by how working with someone has unsettled them into uncharacteristic behavior or deep anxiety. *Every single time* the person in question bears some similarity to a parent, caregiver, sibling, or another significant person from their childhood.

The knock-on effect of drumming obedience into children is that it inadvertently (and, yes, sometimes intentionally) socialized and conditioned us to become adults who distrust our feelings and disassociate from our bodies. We learned to associate *no* with hurting others, confrontation, punishment, and abandonment, hence why we lost our *no* and now feel as if we're disobedient and disrespectful by looking inward. If the person responsible for our care, for nurturing and supporting us, also violated our boundaries, we learned to go toward danger instead of away from it, hence why we might find ourselves drawn to abusive people.

Unquestionably and unconditionally complying with so-called authorities and being expected to prioritize pleasing them might have worked if one thing were unquestionably true: that *all* authorities were loving, caring, trustworthy, and respectful, and that they didn't abuse their power. Obviously, that's not the case.

The Age of Obedience also reinforced the misconception and illusion that compliance is the route to being a Good Person and that complying in and of itself is always a good thing. We've been socialized and conditioned to believe that the world is a meritocracy environment that rewards the version of goodness we ascribe to, and what we've experienced is that this isn't true.

We follow the rules and be and do things the way we've been told, and we still won't be liked by everyone, and we will still experience life's inevitables—conflict, criticism, stress, disappointment, loss, and rejection. We won't always get the job or the promotion, we won't always win over our romantic partner, and even if we tick all the boxes of what we were told would make us good, happy, successful people, we might feel depressed, anxious, disillusioned, or empty. It turns out that being excessively compliant is dangerous to our well-being.

THE TOLL OF PEOPLE PLEASING

My late acupuncturist and mentor, Silvio Andrade, helped me understand what was going on in my body as I was baffled as to why it felt as though I couldn't handle additional stress even though I thought I was okay.

Imagine that, in theory, we're all born with the same stress threshold. We have the baseline of being unstressed, and then we can tolerate a certain amount of stress because we need it as part of our survival to galvanize us when under threat, to adjust to how we're using our bodies, and to alert us when we're overdoing it or when our bodies need something. We need to know when we're under pressure in some way. There's good stress from using our bandwidth in the day-to-day of meeting our needs and enjoying our lives, and there's not-so-good stress that comes from stressors that trigger a sense of threat, whether real or imagined.

So there's the baseline and what we're supposed to be able to naturally and fairly comfortably tolerate, and then a threshold that indicates when we're in high stress. Up until that threshold, we're okay, but after that, our bodies are at an above-average or even dangerous level of stress.

Stress produces the hormone cortisol, and chronic stress produces too much of it, disrupting the body's processes, putting our health at risk, and creating illness.[2]

Sometimes we experience a period of chronic stress that means we're operating close to or above that threshold.

If this continues, the body adjusts to a "new normal," so we'll feel "okay" even though we're not, and we're in this fight-flight-freeze state. If, after this period, we experience an extended stretch of not being chronically stressed and we learn to feel safe and secure again, the threshold will lower.

If, however, chronic stress continues, whether it's because we're still in that situation or we've continued with stressful habits, we will keep pushing our bodies, tolerating far more than we should, and flooding our bodies with cortisol. It's like constantly treading water in stress while overloading our nervous systems and signaling to our subconsciouses that we're under attack.

People pleasing is us responding to anxiety about something, real or imagined, plus it's our response to tension and hoarded anger from our unprocessed hurts and losses. We think those feelings died or that we threw them out in the trash, but they're still there. Some feelings are so buried we forgot we buried them, and piled some more dirt on top! People pleasing is like whack-a-mole, though, because it provides only temporary relief.

Not feeling our feelings, aside from disrupting our emotional intelligence, *also* creates stress. We avoid our feelings to not deal with the stress of something, not realizing that this avoidance is a stressor. And the suppressing and repressing of ourselves to please others means we ignore and distrust our wonderful bodies instead of listening to them. We comply to "keep the peace," not realizing that there's no peace inside us. And because we've gotten so used to being this way, we think we're "fine," not realizing we lost our sense of "fine" and our limits a long time ago.

Much as we might try to behave otherwise, we are not separate from our bodies and minds. When we lie to ourselves, we become at conflict with our bodies. Living our lives with split selves, where we present one aspect to the world and then suppress and repress the other, blocks us from telling our minds and bodies the truth. And so we experience disconnection that manifests as emotional, mental, physical, and spiritual illness.

Many people pleasers beat themselves up for procrastination, seeing it as yet another flawed thing about themselves. Procrastination, though, is like a release valve providing temporary relief from the exhausting habits. Whether we're aware of it or not, and whether we're conscious of how and when it specifically manifests in our lives, it's a form of self-protection. Yes, sometimes we do it because we're delaying and putting something off, but we unconsciously do it as a way of distancing ourselves from all of our *yes*es.

You can't spend all or most of your time doing things from a place of fear and not experience the impact on your well-being. You're not designed to be scared all the time or to be under chronic stress, not only because this prevents you from deciphering when you truly have something to fear but also because being in near constant fight-flight-freeze mode is bad for the business of your body. That's why you either implode by snapping inside yourself and experiencing illness, a breakdown, or burnout, or explode and unleash everything you've been repressing, something we address in the final chapter of the book. Your body has had to go to extreme lengths to stop you in your tracks or make you see what you're carrying.

Although I'm no doctor, it fascinates me that many of my friends and readers who have similar backgrounds or experiences or who people-please similarly have tinnitus, anxiety, IBS, panic attacks, migraines, and mystery illnesses. It's no coincidence that I experienced tinnitus when I went through an extended period of pushing myself to attain, not realizing I was hurting myself by doing it for the wrong reasons and having little sense of my effort limits. It took burning out after running a marathon, losing my father, turning forty, and experiencing perimenopause to go from being frustrated with my "failing" body to using tinnitus as a body signal to help me recognize where I need to listen to myself and say no.

The body doesn't like conflicts and lies. It needs you to tell the truth so you can be okay and well. Appearing as if what you do doesn't bother or hurt you, or take as much effort as it does, or that you are without needs, means people have no idea you're drowning, all while you might feel unseen and unheard. It takes a toll when what you project and portray on the outside is at odds with how you truly feel on the inside.

Never before in the history of humans have we been so exposed, not just to one another, but to this level of noise (audio, visual, sensory, other people's judgment). We're leading lives and repeating patterns that our bodies aren't designed for, hence why we find that the identities we've relied on yield increasingly diminishing returns that leave us confused about what we're "doing wrong" and our "unworthiness." Thanks to technology, we have more of a window into one another's lives than we ever have and numerous means to communicate, share ourselves, and connect. Despite this, we're experiencing unprecedented levels of loneliness, depression, self-harm, teen suicide rates, mental health crises, and burnout.

Sometimes our compliance with authorities means that we blindly trust them and go against our instincts, which can lead to us complying with a doctor instead of seeking a second opinion, perhaps with dire consequences.

Today, workers everywhere engage in presenteeism, performing at being a Good Worker by showing up even when sickness or other factors mean that we're far less productive. It's appearing outwardly compliant while feeling or doing otherwise—passive aggression, a communication style we all engage in at times. We're unwell or disengaged, but we stay late at work; skip breaks; say yes even when we really need to, want to, or should say no; or collapse on the job to tick the boxes of being "present."

Managers, supervisors, and bosses reinforce the presenteeism culture with breathing down our necks, emotional blackmail, and treating us like overgrown babies who can't be trusted with the internet or to manage our time. It's why so many companies claimed that flexible working or working from home wasn't possible, only for the pandemic and its lockdowns to come along and blow those lies right out of the water within hours.

Burnout is significantly on the rise, partly because we now have a word for something humans have long experienced, but also because the increasing demands of work and the difficulty of separating work from our home lives have put a huge amount of stress and fear on us about disobeying and getting into trouble. The exploitative culture of work as a whole is why 2021 was the year of the Great Resignation due to workers quitting their jobs at record rates.[3]

Social media and the internet have made it so much easier for us to compare ourselves, to think we need to be more, do more, and buy more, and we're exhausted by trying to keep up with the expectations.

So many of us are triggered, and the unbearable toll of unconditional obedience on our nervous systems is why we self-medicate and anesthetize with overwork, over- or under-eating, substance abuse, shopping, sex, gambling, and other compulsive behaviors. When we do eventually reach our limits through eruptions and challenges, it can feel horrendous, but this collapse of our false self is necessary if we are to stop being in the pain we pretend we aren't in.

YOUR OPERATING SYSTEM IS OUT OF DATE

Something we have to understand about ourselves is that regardless of having grown up during the Age of Obedience, thanks to how the body works, we were always going to be socialized and conditioned into patterns that we would later on in adulthood have to work to break. Let me explain.

Your subconscious, the part of your mind that you don't have full awareness of, significantly influences your habits, feelings, and actions and operates in tandem with your complex nervous system, which sends signals around your body and responds to your environment.

Think of the subconscious as a mental filing system that's filed (and filing) every single event in our lives and how we've responded. It's like the evidence and case-file rooms that you see in police shows, only vast, given that we have billions of files.

Each file contains details of the event, such as what happened, how we and others responded, and sensory information from the environment. Encasing those details is the emotion associated with them. And this is every event, and although we don't remember most, our nervous systems do.

When you're in a situation that your subconscious and nervous system interpret as being similar to a file or number of files, it triggers you into a sequence of thoughts, feelings, and behavior that will of course pull other files. Even if the event isn't the same as one you've experienced before, if you feel similarly about it, you will respond as though it is (actions, thoughts, more feelings) unless you are conscious, aware, and present.

This means that we are trained to be afraid of certain things for the correct reasons (putting our hand on a hot stove will burn us). However, it also means that based on how we've responded each time we've had to, for example, ahem, say no or have boundaries, we might also be disproportionately afraid of failure or pain even though saying no and boundaries aren't "wrong."

Given the many events in your life, you have unconsciously and consciously batch-filed similar events by using associations, the connections we make between things. I say *salt*, you might say *pepper*. Maybe you think about food or, in my case, start singing Salt-N-Pepa's iconic "Push

It." I mention *no, boundaries, prioritizing yourself,* and something or some-one will spring to mind. A saying, word, emotion, criticism, rule, image of someone, memory, song, smell, physical sensation—*something*.

Humans are creatures of habit. If we had to think out every last thing we do, including the internal functions of our bodies, we'd explode. Joke! But we'd immediately exhaust ourselves. So our bodies do their thing and we build lots of habits, routines of behavior, thoughts, and feelings that automate significant chunks of our days and lives so that we have the bandwidth to focus on anything requiring our conscious efforts.

When we keep responding with the same reasoning habits, feelings, and actions, though, regardless of their truth or relevance, our subcon-sciouses and nervous systems interpret this as the "correct" response, which strengthens and reinforces the contents of that file. So if we say we're "bad" each time we experienced similar feelings to the time our parents snapped at us or we didn't do as we were told, it will become our blanket, *default* response to any and all associated situations, and the feelings will intensify despite it not reflecting our present-day reality and real selves.

But here's the biggie: Your subconscious doesn't tell the time.

Here we are thinking that it's based in the present or even the recent past. Nope! It's based in our early years, so in my case, back in the eight-ies with Jheri curls and frizzy perms (and an epic era of music). And the trap we all fall into until we gain this knowledge and use *no* to wake ourselves up is assuming that our bodies are based in the now and that we should just be able to get with the program. We assume that our feelings are facts and that the stories we tell ourselves about our feelings and our experiences are *also* facts, when they're actually just habits and old misunderstandings.

Understanding that not all the information you hold on file is "correct" is crucial to knowing when and how to respond to the people pleaser feelings, but also reclaiming yourself so that you can trust in you. It's too much to expect that a five-year-old, for example, feels and perceives ev-erything "correctly." If you asked a child to organize your home or do the filing for your business, you wouldn't expect them to do it perfectly, so why continue relying on files that haven't been updated for some time?

YOUR IDENTITY DOESN'T MATCH
WHO YOU REALLY ARE

Much of what we do, especially when unconscious, painful, and repetitive, is about pleasing whomever we depended on in childhood, trying to right the wrongs of the past to meet unmet needs, and protecting ourselves from the rejection and abandonment we feared or experienced as a child. Patterns occur when we're living unconsciously, and people pleasing is us being on autopilot mode. We've been operating from programming instead of preferences.

The amygdala, the part of brain that manages fear, loves patterns so much that it prefers the familiar uncomfortable to the "danger" of the unfamiliar and is ever ready to protect us. That's why much as we might moan about rules, we rely on them because they give us a false sense of control, even though being unconditionally compliant means that we wind up feeling more guilty and afraid.

The part of our brains that stores habits—the basal ganglia—doesn't differentiate between harmful and helpful ones. It clings to all of them, like how my husband tries to hold on to every cable he's ever had even when we no longer have the device to go with it.

The habits of thinking and behavior we default to became *roles*, functions we play in our interpersonal relationships that become our everyday masks and costumes. This "part" that we believed we had to adopt and play was a response to the dynamics of our childhood environments. We made it our jobs to be and do certain things, and we derive our worth from our role(s), using them to fit in and make us feel needed, purposeful, and safe even though, because they're based on childlike reasoning and habits, they also keep us small.

Some of the role will be imposed upon us verbally ("You're the eldest, so you need to set an example!") or via actions (treated like our parents' therapists or substitute spouses or siblings), and some of it we assume (*My parent blames me for everything, so I have to take the fall and be the problem to cover up for them*).

We used the positive and negative associations in our "filing" to work out the "rules" and identify our roles in our families as well as around our peers and authorities. It's like, *If I do X (my role and following the rules), people will do Y (play their part), and then Z (my desired outcome) will happen.* And then we repeated and refined it as we went along, and this programming became our rules for how to live.

No matter how discomforting, limiting, or out of alignment with who we really are, we absorb roles into our identities, not least because we've taken them on to cope and survive, and so they fit the identities of the key people around us. It's our way of "helping out" and "being good" for the greater good of the family. In fact, playing roles is codependency; we're excessively emotionally reliant on others and don't know where we end and they begin. Instead of being more of who we really are, we do whatever we think fits the people around us and our agendas.

And even though we're now grown-up and might be in and around entirely different people and circumstances, in any situation that activates our people pleasing, we still play the role as if nothing's changed in an attempt to meet old unmet needs and right the wrongs of the past.

Our associations and the roles we play explain why we might struggle to understand our challenges or confront our emotional baggage. Social conditioning has taught us what constitutes a "good childhood," so then we dismiss and downplay our experiences or have a major blind spot around acknowledging the journey we've traveled to this point. We might argue, "But my parents are still together!" or "My parents loved me," as if to suggest that only people from "broken homes" or horrific childhoods should, for instance, have low self-esteem or a pattern of unhealthy relationships. But the answer lies in the role(s) we've learned to play.

This doesn't mean people pleasing equals "bad childhood," but "good" or "bad," we still have emotional baggage, and perhaps trauma, to work through. Research shows that adverse childhood experiences (ACEs) significantly impact our lifelong health.[4] Even without an experience on the ACE list,[5] suppressing and repressing our emotions—yep, that would be people pleasing—endangers our health and well-being.[6]

Our coping and survival mechanisms of avoiding *no* with the people pleasing of playing roles helped us get through childhood, but they won't help us thrive, because they're maladaptive. The old programming becomes increasingly inefficient, hence why our people pleasing isn't generating the results or the rewards it used to and taking a toll on our well-being.

This is why saying no, prioritizing yourself, attempting to be assertive, or making much-needed changes in adulthood can feel wrong. It's outside your comfort zone, and as the role has become your identity, breaking the pattern feels disloyal, bad, and disobedient because of its connection to the people you grew up with and what you were taught will make you a good, happy, successful human. You're also afraid that you won't be needed and that you're forcing someone else out of their unhealthy role and inviting further alienation and abandonment. It's like, *Who am I without the people pleasing?* The answer: yourself.

Every day I hear from people who are frustrated with themselves and their lives. They beat themselves up because they think they should have known better or been more resilient or that there's something wrong with them and they're not good enough. But last I checked, none of us woke on our eighteenth birthday to a genie at our bedside welcoming us to adulthood holding a glowing instruction manual on how to do life. How could we possibly find joy in saying no when the world teaches us that saying it is wrong?

So when we're kicking ourselves for what essentially amounts to having emotional baggage that we've never learned how to deal with, never mind how to feel our feelings, meet our needs, and know our values and boundaries; we're ignoring that we've been socialized and conditioned to think, feel, and act the way we do. That's why adulthood is about unlearning all the unproductive and harmful messages we've picked up along the way so that we can become more of who we really are by aligning with our true preferences, principles, and priorities—our values. It's also why you keep coming up against the same problems and feelings: Your subconscious is always trying to make sense of the programming. But if we don't update the operating system by taking responsibility for ourselves and using *no* to heal ourselves with healthier boundaries, our bodies will stick to their defaults.

- There's a "why" in everything we do—our intentions—and knowing why we are doing something helps us live with more conscious intention. When we're aware of our intentions, we enjoy more successful outcomes, whereas when we're not, we deceive ourselves and then feel hurt by the outcomes. Paying more attention to ourselves and our "why" breaks the cycle of *Groundhog Day*–type problems and situations, updating our subconsciouses and nervous systems so that we can take better care of ourselves and understand when we're truly unsafe.
- If complying with something means you can't be an adult and healthily meet your needs at the same time, you need to say no.
- As we can't each automatically see at a glance what the lengths and breadths of a person's boundaries are, the only way in which you can have boundaries is to know and communicate them through what you say and do (or what you opt not to).
- There's nothing wrong with wanting to do things for others, but know your "why." The way you feel, as well as your patterns, outcomes, and results, tell you something about the integrity of your *yes*. You must learn to be responsible for and with your *yes* so that your *yes* doesn't have to be accompanied by decimating your well-being in the process.
- When you people-please, you're responding to the past, not the present. You are not obliged to say yes even when you don't need to, want to, or shouldn't. It's not your *job*.

- Our bodies need conscious input and direction from us to establish new neural pathways and updated responses. We can't keep carrying the same baggage, beliefs, behaviors, and choices into situations and expect a different result and then be surprised when we wind up in the same place, and then lather, rinse, repeat.

So it's time to figure out how your role manifests itself by understanding the specific type of people pleasing you engage in. Whether it's gooding, efforting, avoiding, saving, or suffering, you can start to cut back and reclaim yourself.

PART 2

THE FIVE STYLES
OF PEOPLE PLEASING

Over the years of observing and researching human behavior and relationship dynamics, it's fascinated me that the same patterns come up over and over again as if there's a secret playbook or a Hogwarts for people pleasing. It's so rife, and it goes by other names and descriptions that we don't even connect with the habit.

For instance, in relationships involving emotional unavailability, the more passive partner plays roles to make the emotionally unavailable person eventually spontaneously combust into being emotionally available, willing to commit, or willing to stop mistreating them. Yep, that would be people pleasing.

There's also a trend toward people describing themselves as an *empaths* who are able to perceive the emotional or mental state of another person, without realizing that if what they're doing is without boundaries and feels like a weighty responsibility and duty, what they're describing is people pleasing.

Perfectionist is another way that people who consider themselves very hardworking and high achievers apologetically describe themselves while simultaneously humblebragging because they think it's shorthand for laudable and appreciated qualities. But when it's not so much about being detail-orientated and working to high standards and more about covering up feelings of low self-worth and trying to control the uncontrollable, they're also describing people pleasing.

No matter the description—whether you call yourself a giver or overgiver, overthinker, procrastinator, doormat, over-responsible or over-empathetic, the go-to-person, routinely taken advantage of, misunderstood, the Good Girl, the Nice Guy—these are all different ways of saying the same thing. People pleasing fits into one of five styles: gooding, efforting, avoiding, saving, and suffering. They're about being good and looking good to others, using effort to achieve or to prove ourselves, being avoidant, rescuing people through help and sacrificing one's self, and suffering to prove how good we are or to redeem ourselves, gain acceptance, and be safe. Each style uses the thing it derives value from to influence and control other people's feelings and behavior, attempt to get and avoid the same things by repeating patterns, and try to right the wrongs of the past and nurse old hurts, but from different angles and with different approaches.

Your people-pleasing style offers immediate insight into the ways you do the following:

- Attempt to meet your needs and wants without asking or being direct in your behavior.
- Try to meet other people's needs and desires, and influence and control their feelings and behavior.
- Play roles you've learned and adopted to feel needed, purposeful, or worthy.
- Respond to inner (your) and outer (others') expectations, including obligation, duty, and guilt.
- Still carry pain, fear, and guilt from the old hurts and losses driving your people pleasing.

You might identify with multiple styles, but one or two will dominate. Though I share examples of experiences that can precipitate adopting each style and characteristics of the roles, these can apply in the other styles, so I encourage you to read each one because they're all people pleasing. You'll also recognize loved (and not-so-loved) ones and the roles they play.

The key is to acknowledge what motivates and drives you the most because this will tell you about what you value as well as what you fear— and these will show themselves in the themes and patterns of your life. When you consider what triggers anxiety, worry, or avoidance, and the typical roles you tend to play within your interpersonal relationships, you will see the pattern of what drives you in one of these people-pleasing styles.

Identifying your style isn't about defining and pigeonholing you; it's understanding where you try to fit in and how your upbringing and emotional baggage manifest themselves in how you suppress and repress your needs, desires, expectations, feelings, and opinions so that you can liberate yourself from the pattern.

For example, let's say you cut back on people pleasing at work because it makes you feel like shit and you were doing it to control other people's perceptions. If a coworker tells you they miss the "old," accommodating you, you don't have to roll over and "go back." Of course they miss that version of you—especially if they benefited from it—but they'll live. And probably find someone else to target!

This means that whatever your style of people pleasing and how frequent it is, your people pleasing is driven by hidden motivations. You're not doing something because it represents your true values and intentions and how you feel but because of what you're trying to get or avoid.

> *Remember that what makes something people pleasing is the "why" behind it and how you feel, not how you think it looks, your good intentions, or how others perceive it.*

3

GOODING

When Victoria, a then-thirtysomething senior executive at one of the world's largest companies, overheard her peers gossiping and bitching about management at an internal conference, she reported them for not behaving in a way that upheld company standards. What happened next deeply upset and confused her: Management reprimanded her peers, and as those peers worked out that she was the informant, they distanced themselves and engaged with her only when it was absolutely necessary.

Every day felt torturous for a while, and this was back in the 2000s when working from home wasn't a norm she could escape to. To add to her pain, it had become common knowledge that she'd "grassed them up," and so now her trustworthiness was in question and she didn't look like the team player she'd thought she would. Her colleagues' behavior felt grossly unfair, especially given that she'd been trying to "do the right thing" and be a "good employee," so she couldn't understand how she'd wound up being the Bad Guy.

What Victoria hadn't acknowledged, though, was that in her quest to not just be good but signal this to management, she'd thrown her colleagues under the bus. She'd also wanted to come out with clean hands and anonymity so that she could continue looking and feeling good about herself while enjoying the benefits of an increased relationship with the higher-ups. And not only had this backfired spectacularly, but it also blocked her from recognizing her own inauthenticity, dodgy motives, and lack of empathy for her coworkers.

> Gooding is the image- and reputation-management style of people pleasing that focuses on trying to influence and control other people's feelings and behavior by performing at being a good person to create self-worth and earn the right to meet needs and wants.

While it can encompass aspects of other styles (and vice versa), the primary driver and motivation for gooding is the need to please and be *thought of* as good *in order to* feel secure and worthy. It's more about perception than deeds.

Many people pleasers who'd likely identify with the gooding style of people pleasing can fall into some of the following roles:

The Good Girl/Guy/Something	The Dutiful Son/Daughter
Second Best/The Overlooked One	The Pretty/Popular One
The Successful/Important One	The One Who Has to Be Happy All the Time
The Peacekeeper/Diplomat	The One Who Always Backs Down

THE ORIGINS OF GOODING

A Gooder typically grew up in an environment where the adults modeled goodness even if they didn't necessarily emphasize it, or where keeping up appearances of being good was the priority, or where being good was self-protection against mistreatment from others.

Some arrived at playing their role because they received positive reinforcement for being quiet, being polite, playing nice, not being selfish, being keen to please, not being like someone else who didn't behave as well, going along with things, getting good grades, being popular, or being highly regarded. This created nervousness about disappointing anyone who seemed very invested in their being this way.

When, for instance, their parents suggest the universities they should apply to and visit, the courses they should take, the career they think they're best suited to, whom they should date or marry, and so forth, the Gooder *doesn't* feel as if they can express disagreement. Or, when they contemplate doing anything that deviates from their established identity, they experience anxiety, self-criticism, and indecisiveness that convinces them they're making a terrible mistake. So they stick to gooding.

There are also some Good Girls and Good Guys out there whose appearance, talents, or family shielded them from some of life's unpleasant aspects. People saw the best in them without proof and sometimes exaggerated or outright fabricated their characteristics or abilities. But people also maybe decided that they needed less or that they were more resilient or robust, and so these Good Girls and Good Guys may not have felt they could reveal difficulty or anything that challenged the status quo. While some would argue that it's great for people to think well of you without really having to do anything, when this perception becomes conflated with somone's self-worth and prevents them from being truly seen and heard, it becomes internal pressure to suppress their full selves and play to people's stereotypes, projections, and assumptions.

Other Gooders arrived at playing this role as a response to being inadequately parented and supported, or because they internalized the belief that there was something inherently not good enough about them that they had to compensate for or erase with gooding. In some instances, people assumed the worst about them or had low expectations based on stereotypes, projections, or unfair comparisons—such as assuming they wouldn't amount to anything because of their race, weight, ability, or location—and their whole life has subconsciously been about trying to disprove those assumptions. Because Gooders are essentially trying to fix a problem they don't have (unworthiness or being at fault for other people's feelings and behavior) with a solution they don't need (their own goodness), it reinforces the belief that they're never quite enough.

Even though people haven't necessarily said that the Gooder has to comply, because they've never really engaged in critical thinking about their own needs, wants, and expectations, they experience what can become overwhelming anxiety about not only not doing what others want but also keeping up with people's expectations and appearing happy about it.

It's also safe to say that thanks to the Age of Obedience, some Gooders learned the habit because it's what was modeled or expressly emphasized regardless of what the adults were up to. So if they came from a home where everyone signaled their goodness or kept talking about "good values," they felt obliged to fit in so as not to damage the reputation of the adults. This may be due to religion ("This is a good X household, and we don't do Y") or the adults priding themselves on being a certain type of people or family ("You're a Lue, and that means something. Don't you forget it.").

If the adults were up to no good themselves but wanted to keep up appearances outside the home, wanted their child to make up for their past "bad" deeds, or wanted to keep their child from following in their footsteps, ensuring that their child was obedient and abided by their version of goodness was paramount. It's why we hear, "No one knows what really goes on behind closed doors" a lot, as appearances really can be deceiving. It's also why parents and caregivers may have focused on chastity, limited the child's social life, micromanaged their schedule by cramming it with achievement-driven activities, or stopped them from having friends altogether.

Trying to control a child's goodness to uphold or bolster the adult's reputation or to correct something about themselves makes for an enmeshed relationship where the child is treated as an extension of the adult. When the child complies and meets expectations, the adult and the child are "good," but when the child doesn't or the adult isn't happy in themselves or in control of the universe in spite of their strenuous efforts to control the child, the child is suddenly at fault for wounding the adult's ego.

Families or groups that pride themselves on gooding often close rank when someone deviates or reveals abuse or other no-gooding at the hands of a member. So part of what can teach a person to be a Gooder (or make them fearful of cutting back on people pleasing) is a code of silence, secrets, and shame.

However a people pleaser came to adopt the gooding style of people pleasing, it's been about its effectiveness at limiting or eliminating negative consequences in childhood, such as criticism, physical punishment, being singled out or embarrassed, or being scrutinized. It proved effective at pleasing an expectant, guilt-inducing, or dictatorial parent or caregiver who stressed the importance of being good or keeping up appearances or expected the child to make them happy. In some instances, it also proved effective at *distancing* and *differentiating* the child from that same parent. Often the very people pressuring you into being good are not necessarily the most well-behaved themselves.

While they may have had what they consider to be a "good childhood"—and that's very subjective, as I explained in chapter 2—something in a Gooder's early experiences communicated that being good, obedient, compliant; following rules; and fulfilling duties were intrinsic to gaining attention, affection, approval, love, and validation. The takeaway was that being good was their chief job in life and would not only make them worthy and successful, but would also help out their family in some way. It ultimately taught them that how things appear matters more than how things are and that their value and security lie in pleasing the people who decide if you're good and worthy. Gooders have adopted this childhood message as their expectations and narratives.

This means that although, deep down, a Gooder cares about and craves intimacy, connection, honesty, and loyalty, rather than being "good" from a place of authentically showing up and letting that speak for who they are, they hide their authentic selves and perform at being a good person in whatever the context calls for. They'll do as they're told, follow the rules, or keep up the facade to show how good they are even if they feel and know different on the inside. They will also sometimes invest more in crafting the appearance of being good and claiming good intentions than truly reflecting this in their actions.

Because Gooders cover up anger, control, and hidden agendas with being good and nice, when they experience conflict, criticism, disappointment, rejection, and loss—life's inevitables—they interpret the presence of these as disapproval in and of itself. So it can't simply be a difference of opinion or that someone said no or that they're incompatible. It always becomes an expression of disapproval about how good or worthy or deserving they are. While Gooders are outwardly compliant, they're often silently seething or hurting.

They use people pleasing to buy the credits to stop people from feeling as if they can take issue with them or let them down or stress them out. If and when the Gooder decides to express anger, frustration, or even their belated needs, wants, and expectations, they expect their gooding to be taken into account and for the person to amend their behavior accordingly. Which doesn't happen.

Gooders hate not being liked or any vibe of disapproval, real or imagined. It feels wrong, especially if they don't think it's warranted (they rarely think it is), believe they've ticked all the boxes, and it's someone they admire or whose approval they crave.

They also struggle when it's someone they dislike, even if they won't admit it. Here, it feels particularly offensive and wrong, not least because when Gooders dislike somebody, it tends to be because they don't behave like the Gooder or are being rewarded in ways that seem unmerited to the Gooder. As they pretend to get on with people they feel uncomfortable with or dislike, Gooders don't see why others can't do the same. Given that they spend much of their bandwidth avoiding boundaries and not calling out stuff, it's bound to seem outrageous when other people do.

When someone doesn't appear to understand or care about their gooding ways, or they express disapproval, or the Gooder experiences challenges despite how "good" they've been, it sends them into a tailspin. It triggers genuine confusion, woundedness, indignation, resentment, and sometimes rage.

And so Gooders, like all people pleasers, take life's inevitables to heart because they fly in the face of everything they've told themselves about how they have to be. These challenges, which push them to have healthier boundaries and heal the wounds of gooding, become criticisms and attacks on the belief of the fairy tale of goodness. Their confidence and what they will or won't do is contingent on believing that they are a Good Person almost beyond reproach, and that this is a meritocracy that always rewards goodness, including good intentions and appearing seemingly better than the not-so-good people. Of course, the world doesn't work this way.

YOU KNOW YOUR STYLE IS GOODING IF . . .

- The primary driver of your actions, thinking, and choices is about being positively perceived at all costs.
- You don't say no because of how you think it will make you look (e.g., ungrateful, difficult, bad, disobedient) or because you're a "good" something (e.g., Good Christian, Good Person), or because you think saying no and setting boundaries hurt, inconvenience, or embarrass people.
- You have trouble accepting that someone doesn't like you or that you don't have a good relationship with them despite how good and nice you've been.
- You'll do something you shouldn't (or don't want to) to make the other person feel good or so as not to make things awkward.
- When life doesn't go your way or when people anger, reject, or disappoint you or fail to recognize and validate you, you respond by wondering why it happened to a good person like you, thinking about how you

were merely trying to do the right thing, or feeling you didn't do anything to warrant someone's undesirable feelings, actions, and choices.

- You tell people what you think they want to hear, and sometimes what you want them to hear, to be appealing, to seem similar to them, or to make you both feel good in the moment, which sometimes leads to having to backtrack or go ahead with something.

- You have a strong sense of feeling obligated and guilty and will follow rules, adhere to standards, and comply even when it doesn't feel right, it's unnecessary, you don't have the bandwidth, or it doesn't match your values.

- On some level, you think that you should or will get what you need, want, and expect if you've been or are a good person (or you think you're better than someone you believe isn't as good).

As a Gooder, there's a distinct possibility that, unlike some of the other types of pleasing, you are already aware that you're a people pleaser because you worry, possibly a lot, about pleasing and being displeasing as well as who and what's right or wrong. Even if you don't admit it or have low awareness of it, you really care about what others think. You try to cultivate the right image that signals that you're good in an attempt to control people's perceptions of you so that they will reward you instead of hurting or disapproving of you.

A combination of seeking a sense of self through what others think plus bolstering and securing yourself by measuring and judging your own goodness (and other people's), gooding relies heavily on *should*s and rules to guide thinking, behavior, and choices. It also prioritizes looking good or being good above all else, even when it leads to pain, problems, and losing yourself.

When you struggle to or don't say no, it's because you're afraid that doing so and not continuing with your version of being good will make others (or you) look bad or cause something terrible to happen. It will be as if you said, "Candyman," in the mirror five times, like in the horror film, and now you're looking over your shoulder expecting to be eviscerated.

Rather than being good as part of your values and authentic self, you take on the persona of being good. This takes the form of being a Gooder who sticks fairly rigidly to the same version of being good, almost like paint by numbers or phoning it in or being a chameleon that shape-shifts to whatever you think the situation or person calls for.

You may already have a long-standing track record of being not only good but also rewarded for it and try to maintain or exceed that. Or perhaps you've spent most or all of your life trying to be good but the desired level of recognition, acknowledgment, status, and power has so far eluded you. Either way, it's what you are seen to be doing and how virtuous or positive you perceive yourself to be that you believe will get you the validation and reward you anticipate and desire.

It's the needing your "goodness" to be seen while simultaneously hiding behind the cover of playing roles that forms the backbone of your problems. You're often more concerned with creating the *impression* that things are okay and good than with things *actually* being that way. Gooding takes what can technically be good intentions and deeds and not only turns them into people pleasing because of an underlying agenda and the people-pleaser feelings but sometimes results in your being inadvertently disingenuous, exploiting or putting yourself in harm's way, or overstepping other people's boundaries.

This is what we saw with Victoria because the reality was management knew about her coworkers' discussion only because she mentioned it. And she didn't have to, but the situation activated her sense of goodness, and it was as if it were burning a hole in her pocket. She needed management to see her as good and for them to know that she had not been one of the Others. And she justified her actions to herself because it fit the personas of the Good Girl and the Good Employee. What she hadn't considered was how it fit with her own integrity and how the unanticipated consequences of her actions would feel.

Whatever being "good" means to you, what is actually driving your thinking, behavior, and choices is an underlying anxiety about misstepping and no longer being perceived as good, a desire to prove once and

for all that you are good enough, or a fear of people mixing you up with
One of the Bad Ones. So you strive to be the well-behaved person you
were taught to be or that you think merits approval, and you attach yourself to opinions, behaviors, people, jobs, interests, and lifestyles that are
shorthand for *I'm a good person* and won't invite disapproval and other
negative consequences. This can mean being disingenuous, chameleon-
like, or self-hating.

So many Gooders don't understand why their relationships fail when
they've "been good" by being whatever they thought the other person
needed and wanted and didn't do anything "wrong." They think being
good means being accommodating and deferring by always fitting in
with the needs and wishes of others. This automatic deprioritization and
dismissal, though, is how they wind up feeling neglected, overwhelmed,
exhausted, and resentful. They don't realize that they're not being themselves, and that that's a problem for a partner who wants an intimate
relationship with someone, not with a yes-person. Others tone themselves down to avoid being the Angry Black Woman or the Too-Gay
Gay, for instance, or dim their light so as not to outshine and alienate a
loved one.

While gooding can appear to feel good, you're putting an insulating
bubble around you that prevents you from feeling too much. Being and
doing things to signal that you're a good person might feel good temporarily, but it doesn't make you feel good about yourself because there's a
fear of not living up to the goodness persona by honoring your boundaries. It's also impossible to spend your bandwidth trying to avoid being
bad or attempting to make up for so-called badness and not have a complicated relationship with shame.

Sure, you can praise yourself and take pride in your sense of goodness
or how much you think you've pleased others, but like any people-pleasing
style, gooding numbs you so that you don't have to be too aware of your
own true needs, desires, expectations, feelings, and opinions, or the true
impact of all this gooding.

COMMON THEMES

- Thinking lying is okay if it makes others feel good or fits the image of your being a Good Person.
- Sometimes doing things as a box-ticking exercise so that you can reassure yourself that you're good and succeeding, or to relieve yourself of guilt.
- Assuming that people in certain professions, or who profess to go to church or be religious, or who have noble interests are "good" and share similar values and intentions to you; being inadvertently superficial and drawn to status, popularity, and appearance.
- Choosing your course of study, career, relationship, dwelling, or marriage partner based on what would please family members or what was regarded as socially acceptable or high status.
- Comparing yourself to others and being fearful of misstepping once you're aware of rules or standards, even unrealistic or unnecessary ones.
- Being misconstrued as aloof or superior, for instance because you pride yourself on not getting involved in gossip or office politics or talking out of turn.
- Struggling sometimes to mind your own business, especially when it activates your more moralistic side.
- Having fixed ideas and rules about what you and others should do within a relationship for it to be considered "good" and feeling frustrated and neglected when people don't live up to the picture you've painted in your mind.
- Having a rebellious past that you now try to make up for by living a "good" life, or continuing to lead a double life.
- Basing decisions, big and small, on what will look good to others and how you think they will be judged, so you can find it tricky to contemplate doing something very different from what people have come to expect from you.

STRENGTHS *AND* CHALLENGES

- Following rules and meeting inner and outer expectations without question, especially if it's framed as something to do with being good or the expected, which can make you super-reliable and devoted . . . to the point of exhaustion.
- Placing a high value on being kind, generous, thoughtful, conscientious, giving, and so forth, which means both that you can be very likable and dependable and that truly considering yourself can feel threatening and anxiety inducing.
- Being very attentive and attuned to the needs of others, possibly highly sensitive and empathetic, but this can also make you quite the chameleon as you fit around what you intuit or know, and you can lose yourself and be inadvertently disingenuous.

THINGS TO WATCH OUT FOR

- Imposing your gooding standards on loved ones, and so trying to push them into doing things or feeling aggrieved when they don't pat you on the back for your gooding ways.
- Backing yourself into a corner by using your identity as a justification for why you can't say no or have boundaries full stop, and then martyring yourself. For example, *I'm a Good Christian so I can't tell the invasive and inappropriate member of my church that I'm not interested in dating them and to stop harassing me.*
- Keeping score and being so concerned with what a good job you think you're doing or how you think you come across that you don't ask questions and don't pay attention to what's going on in loved ones' lives or value their contributions.
- Not addressing boundary issues with other people because you don't want to look like a bad person or because you're trying to show them what a good person you are, only for that person to violate your

boundaries or for it to escalate to obsessive or violent behavior toward you or your loved ones.

THE JOY OF SAYING NO:
QUICK SHIFT

- When you find yourself in tricky situations, it's because you've aligned with the identity of gooding, not with who you are. Are you doing this because it's who you are or because you're trying to make people think of you in a particular way?

- Ask yourself: What consequences am I opening myself up to dealing with to avoid saying no so that I look good? For example, eating food you're allergic to or that doesn't reflect your diet to avoid disappointing your parent. Do the consequences reflect the type of relationship you want to have with them?

- Notice where you ruminate about someone not recognizing your goodness and how that influences your subsequent actions and choices—for instance, going into overgiving mode.

4

EFFORTING

Angeline's wanted to stop dating and settle down for several years, but is in her midforties struggling with a disappointment cycle that pushes her anxiety buttons. She meets someone via a dating app; she likes them within three dates even though she also registers "little red flags" that she avoids querying. She thinks it's going somewhere because they "get on so well," or they haven't out-and-out said they're not feeling it. And then she surmises, or they state it when she finally asks or expresses her anxiety about their noncommittal or shady ways, that they're not looking for a relationship.

Instead of stepping away when it's evident that they're not on the same page or that the relationship triggers anxiety-driven habits that derail her self-esteem, she doubles down and feels more invested, as she doesn't want it to end yet. She wonders what she did to put them off when they said they were open to a relationship.

In person, she throws on the Miss Congeniality mask and overgives to demonstrate why they should pick her. Privately, she stops sleeping and eating, and goes into overdrive with work while fighting off thoughts about what she doesn't have, and why, if they can find time to eat or go on social media, they can't reach out or spend time together. The harder she tries, the more she feels entitled to question the situation, raises her concerns or needs, and then backs off when they don't respond how she wants, followed by more effort and more backing off. Angeline doesn't realize her expectations are based on her efforts, not reality or self-respect.

> Efforting is people pleasing that uses effort, achieving, and perfectionism to create self-worth and earn acceptance and safety.

For an Efforter, the primary driver and motivation for their people pleasing is the need to be seen to be *making an effort* and, whether consciously or not, *looking perfect*. They derive value and security from their efforts and recognition of their achievements and accomplishments.

People pleasers who identify with perfectionism, having unrealistic expectations and being self-critical, or being exhausted or near-constantly on the go will likely recognize themselves in efforting and the following roles:

The Overachiever/Successful One	The Straight-A Student
The Over-Responsible One	The Problem Solver
The Strong/Need-Free One	The Good Immigrant/Minority
The Overlooked One/Second Best	The Favorite/Golden Child

THE ORIGINS OF EFFORTING

Efforters were often the eldest, only, unnoticed, under-recognized, or most responsible child. Some Efforters came from efforts-driven families that may have expected them to fly the flag for the family or emulate already high-achieving, accomplished, or hardworking family members or peers. For others, it may be that people around them weren't striving and even discouraged them from overexerting themselves or being too ambitious.

Some arrived at playing their role because they received positive reinforcement for their clear effort, achievements, and accomplishments, and so they learned to derive their worth from performing to a standard, which created a fear of disappointing and failing. It might be that they learned to follow rules, obey, and meet expectations, and they never learned their limits, only how to perform and deliver.

Maybe they were gifted or talented at something, or they consistently got good grades or were rarely, if ever, in trouble. If parents seemed really invested or proud of what they were good at, they assumed it's what made them lovable, making it difficult to stop when they lost interest or wanted to slow down.

Often, Efforters realized that showing up alone wouldn't cut it, especially if somebody had already cornered that market. So if everyone emphasized and affirmed, for example, a family member's beauty or their additional needs, efforting was their way of differentiating themselves.

Others arrived at their role by trying to prove themselves and exert a level of control over themselves and their environment. They were often raised by someone emotionally immature, dictatorial, hypercritical, impossible to please, or narcissistic who may have projected an inflated level of intellect or talent or their unrealized dreams and ambitions, or simply felt that it was the child's job to live up to their expectations.

For some Efforters, failure and slacking weren't allowed, regardless of the appropriateness of the expectations or their bandwidth. Adults may have been quick to temper if they answered incorrectly, got homework wrong, or brought home a less than exemplary report card. There may have been the looming threat of harsh disapproval, physical punishment, disciplinary measures, silent treatment, exclusion, or even abandonment. Meeting standards may have felt like survival as well as their future way out of their environment.

In some instances, while it wasn't specifically said that failure wasn't an option, the adult(s) having an emotional crisis or becoming hostile when the Efforter didn't meet expectations made them want to protect themselves from their reactions. These enmeshed relationships meant they didn't have a separate identity, and so when they performed well, the parent was happy and acted as if it were the result of their efforts. And when they didn't, the parent felt attacked and acted out.

For some, nothing was ever enough. A test came back with a 90 percent score? "Why didn't you get one hundred?" or "Did you cheat?" Or the response was silence or indifference. It was crickets when the Efforter came home from boarding school. Even when praised, there was still some shade ("This is great, but let's see if you can keep this up") or taking credit ("See what my coming down hard on you got you to do?") Any satisfaction was temporary, and then it was back on the efforting hamster wheel again.

Even if criticism wasn't about performance at something, comments about, for example, their attractiveness, personality, and character; name-calling; being compared to others; receiving very little positive feedback due to silence, indifference, or being left to their own devices; or being at the mercy of an adult's moods, whims, and scapegoating taught them to jump through hoops. Efforting controlled criticism, and as they'd learned to dislike or certainly judge themselves due to internalizing this narrative, they now demand too much of themselves as they have little sense of their true limits.

Although it might be out of their awareness, Efforters are competitive and only feel comfortable with their efforts to the degree of awareness they have about other people's. It might come from being compared, for example, to siblings, peers, or even their parent(s), overhearing others being praised, or from being told to be the Best or always give or do their best. They learned to measure themselves against others and pressure themselves to keep up or outdo.

Even if adults don't necessarily say, "You have to work yourself to the bone to be successful," or "Laziness is bad," or even "I'll love or approve of you only if you always meet my expectations," how they behave in the context of effort sets the tone for efforting.

In fact, efforting can be part of a cultural identity that informs how families function within themselves and raise children. It's like a form of good citizenship. The parents make it their duty to make it their children's obligation to excel or have high status or socially acceptable jobs and lives.

Efforting, however, can also be a response to, a side effect of, the immigrant, marginalized, and deprived experience. Work ethic and effort were means of gaining status but also insulating against or limiting discrimination and scrutiny. It managed other people's discomfort and overcompensated for this so-called problematic thing about them so that they could meet their needs and feel worthy. They also internalized society's discriminatory –isms and phobias and weaponized them against themselves. By trying to shake off the inferiority and disprove their laziness or burdensomeness, they're ripe for exploitation and burnout, and it's why they might try to be, for example, the Model Minority, Not-Too-Gay Gay, or Super-Hardworking Fat Person, or mask their neurodivergence or disability.

Efforters internalized the belief that a person's value lies in their productivity, which, incidentally, makes it difficult for them to rest, and even when they do, they tend to feel guilty, agitated, or as if they have to compensate for taking time off by working even harder. They've also internalized an underlying belief that effort is a sign of goodness and that things should go their way if they've made the effort or the most effort, fueling a cycle of unrealistic expectations of perfectionism and also making them most prone to burnout.

Like all people pleasers, Efforters also deduced that their efforting limited negative consequences, especially if they'd seen siblings or peers being punished for underperforming. An overachiever's efforts may have meant that even when they got up to mischief, or they struggled with their physical or mental health, it was overlooked by peers and authorities because of their ability to perform to a high standard. An Efforter maybe concluded that their habits proved effective at making punishment less severe or keeping people off their backs or at a distance.

Although Efforters care about and crave intimacy, connection, honesty, and feeling genuinely good about themselves, they hide behind performing at being the type of person who's making the best possible effort, so rather than operating from their values, they act from a place of insecurity and wind up out of alignment with their needs.

As Efforters tie everything to effort, they interpret experiencing life's inevitables as their not having done enough or people failing to appreciate and reward their efforts. In their mind, their efforts are supposed to insulate them against undesirable outcomes. Given that they've made what they regard as tangible efforts that others use and benefit from, rather than, for instance, focusing on making things look good or avoiding discomfort, they expect acknowledgment and reward. Of course, no one monitors their efforts as closely as the Efforter. This means that once they sense, for instance, that someone doesn't like them, that their romantic interest isn't reciprocated, that something isn't going to come easily (or happen), or that they have a competitor, this activates their efforting and makes them feel invested or owed.

Making an effort is their default setting because not busting a gut feels weird. As a result, they don't like feeling disliked or disapproved of in contexts where they're certain of their effort, where an authority reminds them of old disapproval, or where they believe themselves to be superior to the person expressing disapproval but they wield what the Efforter regards as unearned status and power, which triggers feelings of inferiority.

Efforters really struggle with someone they believe has made less effort having the same or more than them because it blows a hole in their argument for why they do so much.

Feeling rejected or criticized because someone doesn't like their efforts, or assuming disapproval because they haven't received the desired recognition, can prove to be a major blind spot that makes it difficult for the Efforter to receive feedback or to gain the perspective needed to move forward or change course instead of stubbornly persisting.

When Efforters don't receive their anticipated or desired reward and acknowledgment, they feel victimized by their attempts or shortchanged, used, or robbed. In unfulfilling relationships, they overcompensate for the other party's deficit in the hope they'll reciprocate to meet their unmet needs. When they don't, or the relationship ends, they blame themselves. At work, rather than face the real reasons for an issue, they'll effort to try to make the problem go away or get into a protracted battle to prove they're right. Even if they do walk away, they're anxious that someone else is getting what they didn't.

Efforters take failure hardest and hate making mistakes and basically being less than perfect by not meeting their own or others' (probably unrealistic) expectations, which can lead to them wanting to do only things they're sure they can succeed at. They're afraid to make less effort because they hate being wrong about something even though it would set them free. To an Efforter, admitting defeat or that something isn't working equals "quitting."

It's not that something didn't work; they decide they are a "failure" as a person. Because mistakes and failure freak them out, they'll engage in catastrophic thinking that leads to making problematic decisions. They'll hold on to disappointment and rejection by reliving it, like a mourner opting to stay in black for the rest of their days.

Efforters think that the reason they feel so bad about life's challenges is because they're all terrible. While challenges aren't a walk in the park, Efforters put their self-esteem on the chopping block each time they do something and act like someone out there is logging every effort and supposed to be adjusting the universe to manifest only good things. The challenges they experience aren't proof of unworthiness; they're opportunities to break the destructive cycle of efforting.

They regard allowing themselves to be who they really are as something they'll do once they've earned feeling good enough through their efforts. Their confidence and what they will or won't do is contingent on their efforts and the belief that this is a meritocracy that always rewards and prefers people who make an effort. And, of course, the world doesn't work this way.

YOU KNOW YOUR STYLE IS EFFORTING IF . . .

- You focus primarily on using effort to be the Best or to be seen trying hard or proving yourself, gain self-worth, please others, and earn the right to get what you need, want, and expect.
- You don't say no because you don't want to be perceived as giving less than 100 percent; you're afraid of missing out, not being the Best, or looking lazy, incompetent, stupid, selfish, or like you're not a team player.
- You have trouble accepting that no matter how much effort you put in, things might not work out the way you want.
- You feel invested and will continue with someone or something once you're aware of competitors even though it's painful.
- When life doesn't go your way; people anger, reject, or disappoint you; or you don't receive validation and recognition, not only do you try to change the outcome by throwing more effort at it but you also compare yourself, think about your effort and sacrifices and how you did all the right things or were the Best, think you're "a failure" or nothing is ever enough, or feel shortchanged or used.
- You tell people what you think they want to hear (and sometimes what *you* want them to hear) because you're anxious about looking less than perfect, you want to be seen to be making an effort, or you're trying to control the outcome.
- You don't really have a sense of your limits and push yourself to meet other people's and your own unrealistic expectations no matter the cost, including burnout and breakdowns.
- You on some level believe that effort determines whether other people should and will meet your needs, wants, and expectations.

Hello, fellow Efforter! Yes, I'm one too. It's easy to think you're some-one who simply strives to be and do their best. It is people pleasing, though, because if it wasn't, you wouldn't feel uncomfortable about allow-ing yourself to do less and would have a greater sense of and respect for your limits. You inadvertently turn much of what you do into trying to get beyond an A+ on an assignment.

A mix of proving yourself, giving 100 percent, and hoping all your efforts will add up and create a tipping point of reward, efforting relies heavily on unrealistic and made-up, often self-imposed, standards, rules, and expectations to exploit your bandwidth, typically to other people's advantage. It prioritizes being seen to be making an effort at all costs because you associate the amount of effort you make with being a good, worthy, and successful person.

When you struggle to or don't say no, you fear people will think badly of you for not trying hard enough, and it prompts feelings of inadequacy and failure along with fear of missing out on something that could ele-vate your status to the desired level. As you derive your worth and pur-pose from effort, real or potential disapproval of your efforts feels like rejection of you as a person.

Rather than base your thoughts, actions, and choices on your values, you perform at the level of effort that reflects the identity you're trying to project or the reward you're trying to get. So you take on the persona of someone who tries, achieves, accomplishes, or wants the thing, such as Good Employee on the Fast Track for Promotion, the Super-Reliable Friend, Marriage Material, or the Good Dutiful Daughter/Son Who Hopes Their Parent Will Finally Change.

You have a track record of being rewarded for accomplishing, achiev-ing, or consistently giving your best *or* you've spent most or all of your life trying to prove that you're good enough or not lazy, but the desired level of recognition, acknowledgment, and so forth hasn't happened yet. Whatever the situation, you want to be seen as making an effort. Or, at the very least, you expect the effort you've made to count when people judge you, determine whether you've earned something, or decide how they're going to conduct themselves.

For you, the more effort you make, the less disapproval you believe you should experience and the more likely it is that something will or should happen. And this is how you make the rod that eventually breaks your back because your solution to anything that activates your people pleasing is to *try* harder. You veer between acting as if you have zero needs or are low-maintenance and then feeling needy when you're not rewarded. While you regard meeting other people's needs as an imperative, your own are often treated like rudimentary, nuisance tasks to sideline or tick off in the pursuit of goals and putting in effort, not a means of taking care of and respecting yourself and your relationships. You can have an *It doesn't matter how you feel* attitude toward yourself and others when you've decided something has to be done or endured. When you don't keep your efforting in check, it becomes like trying to brute-force and white-knuckle life into bending to your will, and you don't know when to back off.

Angeline, who's crazy about her efforts, not her dates, doesn't do things because it's authentically her but because she's trying to steer the situation to her desired outcome. She goes into autopilot the moment she feels interested, which is typically set off by *anxiety,* not genuine interest. From there, she bases her expectations not on the true nature of the situation but her efforts, which reflect her already being the girlfriend even though the person behaves otherwise. It's all about building a case for a relationship by being the Good Girl Who's Done Everything Right and then feeling owed, hence why partners feel manipulated and pressured, and why she feels increasingly anxious due to repeatedly going against herself.

Clearly, trying is no bad thing, but don't confuse it with anxiety and self-neglect. Again, it's the "why" that makes your efforts people pleasing. There's a world of difference between the trying that happens when pursuing a particular accomplishment, and the trying used to cover up underlying feelings of low self-worth and to generate or even speed up a desired outcome. The former leaves you with room to say no, and the latter causes you to say yes for the wrong reasons.

You assume you try only where effort is required or that wanting or needing something is the sign that effort is required, but in reality, you overgive and overdo it regardless of who or what the situation is. Not only does this lead to exploiting yourself (and allowing others to do that to you), but it enters people into contracts they don't know they're on the hook for. You expect from others, not based on who they really are but what you do, and whether that's who you expect them to be or how you expect to be rewarded, it oversteps boundaries while setting you up for pain.

You think you're giving 100 percent and proving yourself, but what you're doing is being so afraid of disapproval and not getting what you want that you overcompensate by trying to give *beyond* 100 percent so that you're above reproach and less likely to get hurt. Even if you're not actively trying to be perfect and think you're merely trying to be "good enough," you're trying to be the perfect version of good enough.

Efforting with all its perfectionism and exploitation is a form of hiding that, like all people pleasing, stops you from thinking and feeling too much because you don't know who you are without the doing. But if you don't allow yourself to feel, you lose yourself in the doing and won't realize when you're way over your limit.

COMMON THEMES

- Pride in being friends with all of your exes or not having fallen out with anybody.
- An attitude of earning rest and self-care and then almost paying it back with more effort, hence why you might skip meals, sleep, or bathroom breaks or only realize how hungry, tired, desperate for the bathroom, or ill you are when it's become urgent.
- Under-earning because you work so many more hours than you're paid for, effectively reducing your salary.

- Taking over, sometimes because you think the other person or people are incompetent, in other instances, because you struggle with not having control; perhaps not trusting people to do their part.
- A disproportionate fear of missing out on being asked to take on something (favor, task, project) or of burning bridges. You don't realize that you're sometimes afraid of missing out on the opportunity to be exploited. You get offended or insecure when not asked even if you don't want to do it or you don't have the bandwidth.
- Moving on quickly from accomplishments and not internalizing your efforts; perhaps feeling insecure without praise and affirmation, leaving you with imposter syndrome feelings of being a fraud and not having done enough.
- Overdoing it on projects and tasks because you focus on your perception of your efforts, fear of failing, or trying to be perceived in a certain way, which can cause you to misunderstand briefs, objectives, and responsibilities.
- Regarding illness, even one caused by your efforting, as an inconvenience or failure, and feeling guilty about letting people down or them having to, for instance, do your work in your absence or step up more than they usually do.
- Having a long list of things you want to do but don't think you have the time for or that you think you need to or should be doing because you think they'll make you a better person.
- Exhausting yourself before taking time off because it's as if you think the place will collapse in your absence or that you're afraid people will find out something about you or decide that they don't need you.

STRENGTHS *AND* CHALLENGES

- Placing a high value on delivering and being reliable, conscientious, a hard worker, not lazy, and so forth, so you have the ability to throw your heart and soul into pretty much anything, but you resist asking for help or giving off signs that you are struggling. Not only does this create a false impression of what goes into your efforts so that incidentally others will expect them as the norm from you, but it leads to blood, sweat, tears, and burnout.

- Following real, arbitrary, and self-imposed rules and complying with outer expectations, often without question, especially if there's a clear goal or perceived reward or it activates your need to win or to prove something, which can make you the go-to person for getting things done. The lack of discernment, though, puts you out of alignment with your values and can be exploited by more aggressive and manipulative people.

- Expecting a lot of yourself and pushing yourself to meet inner expectations, which means that you can accomplish a hell of a lot and be highly regarded by others, but it also means that you don't have a sense of or respect your limits, you have unrealistic expectations, and you suck the frickin' joy out of just about anything due to your feelings about "failure" and being "good enough."

THINGS TO WATCH OUT FOR

- Being so focused on achieving a goal, winning, having the last word, or getting the person to come around to your way of thinking that you let your ego get the better of you or you don't really get to enjoy anything.

- Treating loved one's efforts as a reflection of you, so feeling as if you have to have a high-achieving child, partner, friends, or family, and then feeling ashamed or micromanaging them if they are not. This might include dragging them toward your dreams and calling them "their" dreams.

- Staying in unfulfilling relationships and situations long past their sell-by date because you think it reflects poorly on you that you couldn't make it work.

- Striving to make things look easy, even when they're not and even when you shouldn't be doing the thing in the first place, and then feeling overwhelmed, neglected, and resentful because people can't see how much you're struggling even though, from the outside, you're like a swan, calm on the surface while furiously padding underneath.

THE JOY OF SAYING NO: QUICK SHIFT

- Dial things down by trying to identify what you think doing something at 70 percent would look like. I know, I know. I felt a shudder in my tummy when I first started doing this. But your idea of 100 percent is more like 150 percent, so you need to get a more realistic sense not only of your limits but also of whether everything requires that full-watt, bust-a-gut level of effort. There's plenty of stuff in your life that requires a fraction of this effort.
- Ask yourself: Am I in a situation that genuinely warrants my level of effort, or am I anxious and trying to control or manipulate something?
- Make it an automatic *Let me get back to you*. You are the people pleaser who is likely to overcommit, overwhelm, and overextend yourself, so you need to make a concerted effort to check your schedule, bandwidth, desire, and necessity to do something.

5

AVOIDING

Marcus always knew he was different from the rest of the family, but according to them, he wasn't adopted. Given that they were white and he was black, he knew there was clearly a backstory to his conception, but no one talked, so he didn't either.

He said they didn't treat him any differently and were a close-knit family, so he threw himself into excelling at everything and ensuring he never let himself get "too emotional" lest it unleash something he couldn't control and upset everyone.

His cooperating with the obvious secret later baffled partners, with them often citing the toll it took on him as a reason for him to address it, which led to him distancing or cutting off. When the sense of loss, confusion, alienation, and secret resentment bubbled up, feelings he couldn't register or compute but knew to avoid, he threw more work, humor, and then drugs and alcohol at it. Any partner who stuck with him understood to mind their own business, acknowledging how delicate an issue it was.

But then the pandemic hit. He had to work from home, the usual bars and clubs weren't open, and he couldn't disappear for hours, sometimes days on end, and everything came crashing down, including his marriage, where his partner hit a wall with his unreachableness and substance abuse. And so after more than fifty years of being mommy's Good Little Boy, he finally asked her who his father was, a question he, in theory, could have asked all along, but was afraid and had, instead, designed his entire life around avoiding.

> Avoiding is the style of people pleasing that uses evading, hiding, merging, and blending as a means of pleasing others and meeting needs and wants.

Although Avoiders have gooding or efforting traits, the primary driver for everything is *avoiding discomfort and their fears*. So, a sense of work ethic, for instance, or proving themselves wouldn't drive their overwork; their motivation, even if they're unaware of it, is avoiding dealing with *something else*. They'd be agreeable, not to keep up appearances but to avoid triggering the apocalypse they believe would happen if they were honest.

People pleasers who tend to blend into the background or who've coasted with more assertive and aggressive emotionally unavailable people may recognize themselves in one of these roles, especially if a recurring theme is avoiding expressing feelings, talking about issues, or struggling to make decisions and commit.

The Dreamer	The Shy/Quiet One
The Lost/Overlooked One	The Underachiever
The Super-Busy One	The Listener
The Entertainer/Comedian/ Butt of the Joke	The Fringe Player

THE ORIGINS OF AVOIDING

Avoiders typically grew up in an environment where avoiding was what everyone did, being different meant needing to hide it to stay in their family, or circumstances meant avoidance became an effective strategy for self-protection.

They received praise (or certainly positive, not negative or neutral, feedback) for avoiding difficult subjects, not expressing feelings, being need free, not asking for help, not causing problems, and maintaining the status quo. It made them fearful of intimacy because the unfamiliarity of closeness and running the risk of conflict felt intense and threatening.

Some arrived at playing their role because not dealing with things was considered polite or the means to keep their place in the family. There might not be a Big Family Secret or a scandal; things may have been pretty uneventful or at least appeared to be. When a child can't even talk about or is limited to the small things, though, they're unlikely to feel confident about voicing bigger things or revealing themselves. Or, when no one asks questions or goes beyond surface level, even the most innocuous questions become weighty.

Their parents maybe never exchanged a cross word or displays of affection, or emotions were a rarity. Though everyone appeared to get along, the Avoider felt lonely, neglected, unsure of themselves, or afraid to be too much of themselves.

Although it wasn't necessarily explicitly stated that certain topics were off-limits or that, for example, asking for help or expressing feelings were bad, keeping things surface level, walking on eggshells, and the *absence* of conflict, emotional expression, and discourse communicated that going along to get along was the way to be good and okay.

So, for instance, older siblings or relatives may have chastised a younger child for emotional displays and even suggested that their behavior made the parent ill or upset. Or they experienced bullying or struggled with an eating disorder or something else and didn't feel as if they could confide in family, or when they did, some were in denial or accused them of "acting out" and "looking for attention."

Some Avoiders describe their backgrounds as "happy homes" or "idyllic childhoods" with "loving" and "attentive" parents who "never laid a hand on them." But in response to low feelings or struggles with difficult events or their sense of self, their parents stressed focusing on the positive and not dwelling too much. Or their parents were distressed as to why the child felt unhappy despite everything they had provided or how they tried their best to be a good parent. So as children Avoiders learned to hide the difficult aspects of their life and avoid rocking the boat to show gratitude and please their loved ones.

Of course, plenty of Avoiders maybe feel like all people did was express themselves. Maybe there was lots of fighting, or one or a few voices dominated. And so now they play it small to keep the peace and for self-protection.

Although for adults, screaming and shouting, name-calling, threats, throwing stuff around, talking through gritted teeth to try to disguise yet another about-to-be argument, slamming doors, breaking up to make up, or being physically abusive toward each other may have felt like an average day, as I can attest, it's bloody terrifying for a child to witness, overhear, or even be caught in the middle of.

Whether sitting in the car as an argument escalated, hiding under a table, or trying (or feeling powerless) to protect a sibling, parent, or themselves from the aggressor, they developed very negative associations with conflict and criticism and became hypervigilant. While a child might learn to manage overarousal of their nervous system with the likes of efforting, their hypervigilance might manifest as avoiding where they're often unconsciously assessing the perimeter for signs of potential conflict. They learn to numb themselves to feel safe and in control.

Perhaps the Avoider was overshadowed and learned to take a back seat. One person's moods and problems may have dictated the dynamic and took precedence. The person may have done all the talking and thinking for them or become hostile and emotionally blackmailing when disappointed. Or, the Avoider made it their job to stay out of the spotlight. This dimming of their light means that even though they're now a grown-up, part of them fears alienation or abandonment if they grow, hence why they might hold themselves back romantically or in their career, but also why they have imbalanced relationships where, for instance, they always play the role of the Listener or Mediator.

It's not as if they want to be up in people's business like, say, a Saver or Gooder might, but being in the middle or taking a back seat takes the heat off. They might feel distinctly *un*comfortable with, for instance, someone unloading on or involving them, but not expressing this protects them from becoming the target of conflict.

And some learned avoiding from a trauma, conflict, or loss that made them shut down and stay in the shadows. They associated whatever happened with confrontation, with being too honest or vulnerable, and so avoided, not simply to numb painful feelings and limit further fallout, but to protect themselves from ever being in that situation again.

For instance, maybe it was their parents' breakup or divorce and feeling caught between them, or an acrimonious split permanently changed the family. A significant bereavement and not understanding the circumstances or feeling abandoned or even blaming themselves can also teach someone not to rock the boat.

I've heard from many Avoiders where their parent leaving or dying before they were born or in the early years has never been discussed. It might be not wanting to upset the surviving parent or cause an argument, especially if the parent became withdrawn, disinterested, or, at the other end, angry and resentful. Some Avoiders tried, only to be chastised or punished, or the parent claimed sudden illness. Or perhaps the adults felt it best not to dwell. Some Avoiders knew part of the backstory and felt ashamed or abandoned, or the mother didn't know who the father was, or they did but withheld the information. And for children, what they don't know in these situations, they make up, and it's always worse than the truth.

Sometimes it was the child knowing about, for instance, affairs, criminal activity, or substance abuse. Or someone was in prison, rehab, or an institution, but the pretense was that they were on a long-ass holiday, again.

The Avoider may have experienced abuse or been aware of someone else's, but there was a code of silence and even the threat of expulsion from the family. It may be that the Avoider suspects that their parents or caregivers know about the abuse they experienced but have chosen not to confront it, and so they don't confront it either, and it's become their generalized pattern of pleasing others.

An Avoider can appear high functioning or as if they're coasting along not bothering anyone while privately struggling. They play their cards very close to their chest and design their lives to avoid dealing with their fears and feeling too much.

Let's be real: The culture didn't accommodate self-expression or even value the importance of feelings and how numbness, secrecy, shame, and trauma events take a major toll on our well-being until very recently.[1] Whether silence, neglect, or violating boundaries, these were generational patterns and the family unit's response to unprocessed trauma. Even if therapy was involved, the attitude may have been to fix the child, not to fix a family issue. Some Avoiders were yanked out of therapy when the therapist pointed out the real problem or family treated the Avoider with suspicion about what they might be disclosing.

While all people-pleasing styles control disapproval by limiting or avoiding life's inevitables, Avoiders avoid anything that will make things harder on anyone else, so it also involves controlling attention, affection, approval, and even validation and love.

They too use their people pleasing to buy the credits to avoid negative outcomes, so when they experience conflict, criticism, and so forth, even though they've done their utmost to ward it off, it feels scary as hell and as if they've failed because they're realizing their fears. Then they up the ante on avoiding.

Because everything's a strategy for avoiding fear and they want to be middle-of-the-road to stay in their comfort zone, it can take quite some time to come face-to-face with an issue or they might go around in circles, especially as they might stonewall, overgive, and overthink to get out of dealing with something.

Although all people-pleasing styles involve passive aggression, the others, when push comes to shove, will deal with something, even though they might struggle. Avoiders will try to run out the clock by trying to stall the inevitable confrontation or going into overgiving mode in the hope of sidestepping the issue. When things go awry, they justify their avoidance by claiming that the person's response or the disappointing outcome is proof it's best not to talk about or deal with something, and will also feel owed because of their "pleasing."

The buildup of fear and being constantly on guard triggers catastrophic thinking in their close relationships where they panic that the person will leave when all they want to do is try to get to the bottom of the issue. Because they go along with things, when someone expresses discontent, the Avoider feels criticized or rejected and reminds the person that it was "their idea" or "their dream." They won't get why something is happening because they rationalize that they were doing what's best or that it's not a problem because they went along with the other person's agenda, which creates further friction because the Avoider won't take responsibility for their part in things. In situations where they sense that they're going to get hurt in a way they think they won't be able to handle, they might opt out first, disappear, or finally erupt, much to everyone's surprise, including theirs.

Avoiders believe that everyone shares their fears and also wants to avoid them in the same way. They genuinely believe that avoiding is a good thing that people will and should be pleased by. But avoiding makes it difficult to form new relationships with people who require more intimacy and honesty. It also means that it's their default to enter into situations with avoidant habits regardless of whether there's a threat, and so they're inadvertently braced for the worst without recognizing how their avoidance creates far more problems than it solves.

YOU KNOW YOUR STYLE IS AVOIDING IF . . .

- The primary driver of who you are and what you do is minimizing or outright avoiding conflict, criticism, and making others uncomfortable.
- You don't say no because you think it causes more problems than it solves and are trying to avoid any and all forms of negative consequences.
- When life doesn't go your way, people anger, reject, or disappoint you, or you don't receive validation and recognition, you're mad at them for bringing something up or taking issue with you given all the things you let slide; you try to act as if you're not bothered or it didn't happen, or you distance, ghost, or cut them off.
- You tell people what you think they want to hear because you have little or no idea how you really feel or think, or you do but fear being wrong or unappealing, or you want to hastily shut down your discomfort or move on.
- You play it small as a strategy—for instance, by hiding out in work or in unhealthy or unfulfilling relationships—to fit with other people's expectations of you so that you don't upset or alienate them by changing or getting "too big."
- You believe that not talking about anything that makes you or others remotely uncomfortable, keeping the peace, and sweeping boundary issues under the carpet is a good thing and should be rewarded.

It's possible you were unaware that your avoidance of discomfort was part of a people-pleasing strategy for acceptance and security because by the very nature of avoiding, you're not going to think too deeply about your motivations or anything for that matter.

Using elements of other styles of people pleasing but with the primary aim of keeping discomfort to the absolute minimum, avoiding makes your life a delicate balancing act of trying to keep people sweet while pretending this isn't what you're doing or that it's not causing problems. You derive your sense of self from how successfully you manage to maintain the illusion of everything being your version of okay and how safe you feel, so you will try to be in situations where, in theory, given that you become what you think a person or situation calls for, you should be okay. After all, why reject someone who is the same or doing what's expected? It's a form of perfectionism that allows you to hide.

When you struggle to say no or don't say no it's because you fear being unable to deal with the consequences. You think it will be like opening Pandora's box, and a lifetime of avoiding and limiting *no* has only heightened your fear. You want to keep this person sweet so that you don't invoke their anger, real or imagined, and burst the illusion, and so, ultimately, there's a fear that if you express yourself fully, you will invite rejection, disappointment, and conflict into your life.

For you, being good means never discomforting people, and so you take on this perfect persona of someone who can handle everything or who doesn't need very much and is happy to go along. You have to pretend you know less than you do and make it a professional sport to be passive. You learned that telling or knowing the truth would not be okay, so it's better to avoid it, and now you're so proficient at telling people what they want to hear, you don't even know it's a lie. As a result, you are a dangerous combo of too nice, nonconfrontational, and naive that disguises a guardedness where you're quietly waiting for the other shoe to drop.

All your life you may have been getting by on keeping people sweet, so you have little experience with healthy conflict resolution or facing things head-on, or you're still trying to prove that avoiding is the best way to go after becoming worn out with people and experiences that were too confrontational.

Needing to avoid discomfort, your own and other people's, is, ironically, the fundamental cause of your own unacknowledged discomfort and the need for you to clean up your messy side of the street in issues that arise. You're like the boiling frog who doesn't know they're boiling until it's too late. While you have a low tolerance for risk, you have a high threshold for pain, and so you deny, rationalize, minimize, excuse, and assume to keep the illusion of "okay" alive only to then have to anesthetize in some way or be passive-aggressive to express or numb the feelings you don't even know you're avoiding.

Marcus and his family thought they were doing the right thing, but he paid a high price for not being able to admit that everyone else was in on something he wasn't. He went along with the pretense to love and protect them while simultaneously hating and not knowing himself. And avoiding begets avoiding: Avoiders can't be in anything too real because it messes with the other aspects of their life that they avoid, and so you can inadvertently sabotage your happiness to maintain the status quo.

If there's an issue, it means things are not "perfect," so you try to avoid dealing with it to keep up that illusion, confronting it only when you feel sufficiently disillusioned and resentful. You people-please to try to almost make the other person perfect in your mind, and so when they piss you off or let you down, you feel rejected. Sometimes you shock people because you keep your reservations, discontent, and hurt to yourself, acting like everything is hunky-dory and giving zero indication that something is wrong, communicating it only when you melt down, announce you're breaking up or leaving your job, or stop speaking to the person.

You might be one of the nicest people anyone could meet, but it all comes from a place of disowning yourself if there's so much as a whiff of the potential for discomfort, and people don't realize for some time that you avoid saying or doing anything that might give someone too much of an opinion of you. By sometimes being too bloody nice for your own good, not realizing it's coming from avoidance, plus avoiding confrontation and feigning naivete and sometimes confusion, you become subsumed by the people in your life. You accommodate everyone and defer to them, putting you on the fringes and making your sense of identity fragile due to your dependency on the situation being perfect.

It can feel so wounding when a relationship or situation doesn't work out because you genuinely think going along to get along and avoiding were the best way to please the person and not endanger what you wanted. But not only are you walking on eggshells as a default, you don't realize how people consciously and unconsciously feel they have to do that with you.

There's a time and a place for avoiding something when you're in actual danger or where there's a genuine benefit to delaying something for a time before dealing with it, but what you're doing is avoiding and postponing yourself. The people you learned avoiding from had their own stuff to deal with, but why should they get two lives (yours and theirs) while you don't have yours?

COMMON THEMES

- Lying to absolve people of their need to feel concerned even though you might be really struggling and will later feel neglected by their not instinctively knowing something was wrong or what to do without your telling them.
- Going along with something wrong by staying silent even though it can mean big problems for you or others. It's not that you agree with, for example, bullying or exclusion, but your fears overwhelm you, leaving you feeling bad about yourself but also sometimes getting you into trouble as result of appearing to have colluded in the problem by not doing anything.
- Ghosting, avoiding, or cutting people off instead of being honest or dealing with things, and possibly attempting to reconnect and glossing over things as if nothing happened, or responding by glossing it over when someone does that to you.
- Keeping your friendships surface level so that they don't know too much about you or need too much from you, or so that when they disappoint you, it's easier to back away and not have to have a conversation.

- Avoiding certain people you feel uncomfortable around so that you don't have to say no and bolting when you see them, claiming you didn't hear them calling you or that you have bad eyesight or something.
- Priding yourself on never fighting with a partner or with anyone.
- Backing away from ideas if you sense that people are not in agreement, even though they might have no clue what they're talking about or they're not even your target audience.
- Erupting in anger, hurt, and frustration after systematically tolerating the unacceptable and then feeling ashamed and retreating back to avoidance.
- Taking long breaks from relationships after getting hurt as an emotional purgatory and then becoming involved in fantasy relationships or an intense and unhealthy relationship, only to get disappointed again and then retreat.
- Going into overdrive to avoid dealing with something. For instance, you know that there's an issue, so you throw gifts, good deeds, or compliments at it so that the other person (hopefully) feels awkward about bringing it up. Or, you turn to alcohol, substances or some form of compulsive behavior to escape your feelings and the situation.

STRENGTHS *AND* CHALLENGES

- Being good at smoothing ruffled feathers and not getting into unnecessary conflicts, but you also won't get into necessary ones and will go so far as to sell your soul if it means not having to deal with other people's feelings or with conflict or criticism.
- Thinking out big (and sometimes much smaller) decisions to the nth degree and playing out situations in your mind, but this often results in overthinking and delaying tactics that trigger paralysis, stonewalling, or vacillating, much to the chagrin of anyone waiting for you to get off the fence.

- Coming across as a good listener and empathetic because you volunteer so little of what's going on in your own world, so people will trust you with their problems and secrets, but this can leave you feeling dumped on, drained, and neglected and may cause you to distance yourself.

THINGS TO WATCH OUT FOR

- Overthinking by dwelling on things for too long, trying to work everything out perfectly in your head before you'll make a move, or making up stories that find fault in you when, for example, you see that someone's in a bad mood.
- Not having any real interests or close relationships of your own because you do whatever your partner or sibling wants and then feeling resentful when they ask you to suggest something or want to do something without you.
- Casting people as "troublemakers," "difficult," "needy," or "too sensitive" because they express their feelings and don't want to shove issues under the carpet or go to therapy.
- Gaslighting people by insisting that nothing is wrong when there is indeed an issue you're avoiding, and projecting your feelings or perceptions about yourself or them and then calling them their feelings.

THE JOY OF SAYING NO: QUICK SHIFT

- Gently test out your comfort zone. Imagine how you feel about doing something on a scale of 0 to 10. Someone at a 10 would be able to comfortably handle what you feel uncomfortable about. Where are you on that scale? Let's say you're a 3. What would someone who is a 3.5 or 4 do? Do that. Don't try and do what you think is a 10, as it will likely trigger deep anxiety.

- Ask yourself: Am I doing this because I have actively, consciously chosen to, or because I'm trying to avoid conflict, criticism, intimacy, *something*?
- While being analytical undoubtedly has its uses, it's no substitute for action, so be careful of where you overthink, try to anticipate the future, or try to work out everything in your mind before taking a step to avoid dealing with or making a decision.

6

SAVING

Gaby has spent most of her adult life caring for family members and picking up the slack of anything they don't want to deal with. As a result, romantic relationships are few and far between and she parked her career and dreams to step in. When she's had romantic relationships, they've been with wounded souls with whom she winds up feeling like their mommy or their plaything, so she's been in a fantasy relationship for nearly a decade with someone who's perennially unhappy and wants to meet only once in a blue moon.

When Gaby became so unwell that she had to go on bed rest, her sister still expected to drop off her children most days, and family seemed most concerned about when she was going to be back up and running. Even though her siblings could have stepped in, she still tried to care for her mother, but found this exacerbated her symptoms and that it felt like her family were draining her life force. As months went by with minimal support, Gaby's anger and hurt mounted at having sacrificed her adulthood for her family. She realized that nobody was going to help her because they saw helping as *her* job.

As she grappled with the injustice of it all and the grief at who she could have been, she gradually acknowledged that while her family's behavior was problematic, she had also made saving them her job by dropping everything, refusing to say no, and enabling their behavior. She had, in fact, used her family as an excuse not to pursue the things she was scared of and to prove, once and for all, that she was needed by them.

> Saving is people pleasing where the person tries to be the solution to other people's problems by taking on their responsibilities, and "giving" through fixing, helping, and rescuing in order to feel needed, purposeful, and valuable. It's the "at your service" style of people pleasing.

While Savers use gooding or efforting traits to facilitate their saving and are secretly avoidant, the primary driver and motivation for their people pleasing is the *need to be needed* or to be *seen to be needed* to feel secure and worthy. They try to influence and control other people's feelings and behavior with "help" and shouldering responsibility at the expense of themselves.

Anyone who's noticed that their relationships feel imbalanced and possibly one-sided, or who's felt burned and worn out from being there for others, will recognize themselves in saving and the following roles:

The Fixer/Healer/ Rescuer/Savior/Hero	The Substitute Parent/Spouse
The Avenger	The Strong One
The One Who Does Other People's Dirty Work	The Therapist
The Rebound	The One Who Takes the Blame

THE ORIGINS OF SAVING

Savers grew up in an environment where being of service was modeled or emphasized, where children shouldering what were likely adult responsibilities was the norm, or where the adults were not in a position to help themselves, never mind their children.

They received praise or positive feedback—attention, affection, and so forth—for being good, caring, and accommodating via helping, fixing, rescuing, saving the day, selflessness, having it "together," or needing less than others, and learned to derive their purpose and value from meeting the needs of others, so they didn't get to develop a self outside of what they did or do for others.

Savers likely had to take on way too much responsibility in childhood, or assumed that they had more power over people's happiness than they did, or felt as if they'd failed to save someone significant.

Of all the pleaser styles, Savers are most likely to misunderstand their pleaser efforts because of being well-intentioned but also the lengths they may have gone to provide help and support, and so they feel especially confused about boundaries due to the particularly codependent nature of their relationships and their giving.

Growing up in an environment where they inadvertently learned that sacrificing and exploiting yourself to help others in need is "giving" means that they don't know their responsibility, so it's tricky to know their boundaries because they're over-responsible. Learning or teaching themselves that fulfilling someone else's responsibility or need is "helpful" and "not selfish" means they've spent all or most of their lives feeling guilty for having a self and then almost trying to give it away to prove their goodness.

Some Savers came to their role because a parent or caregiver modeled saving, possibly martyrdom. And because they loved that parent and thought (or were taught) that what they were doing was the right thing for a person to do or what, for instance, a Good Spouse should do, they've adopted this blueprint as their own. Repeating the role is a form of loyalty, and they may feel bad about doing anything that hints at selfishness. Conversely, though, the Saver may have seen the flaws in the adult's saving, still copied it, but tried to be successful where their parent wasn't. The Saver wasn't necessarily given adult responsibilities, but it was stressed in some way that to be good was to help by giving of themselves.

Some came from a gooding-type environment where keeping up appearances was emphasized, but in the hope that you were seen as someone who was of service and always helping others. Some came from a more efforting-leaning environment where helping others was also paramount but the emphasis was on what might be backbreaking, sacrificing effort, such as giving up comforts or going without to help others.

It can be that adults projected an older persona onto the Saver, possibly by talking about deeply inappropriate subjects and/or confiding their woes in the child. Emphasis on being the eldest or how they were "mature," "wise," or an "old soul" caused the Saver to forget they were a child. If a child appeared to manage things easily, didn't cause trouble, or seemed okay on their own without much help or intervention, the parent's attention may have been diverted to others with seemingly greater needs, or they may have assumed the child needed less and involved them in adult jobs or decisions.

Other Savers came to their role because they grew up too soon by having to take on adult responsibilities. They may have helped raise siblings, acted as a substitute spouse whether it was single-parent household or not, or cared for a parent or caregiver who, much as they may have wanted to, wasn't in a position to due to, for instance, illness, disability, working long hours, being a caregiver, or struggling with grief or addiction.

In other instances, the parent or caregiver didn't want to take responsibility, or they believed it was the child's duty to help with adult responsibilities, possibly because they themselves were raised that way. Or, the adult may have been pursuing their life at the expense of parenting. The Saver then learned to step in where the adults couldn't or wouldn't, adopting an over-responsible identity for their own survival and possibly that of their siblings or even caregivers. The Saver developed a sense that the people around them wouldn't survive without the Saver, which later created a generalized feeling of people not being able to manage without them.

The Saver may have felt a deep sense of responsibility to protect their parent or caregiver by covering up their deficiencies. It may have been to spare the adult(s) from shame or to try to support them enough that they might eventually get the energy to be able to parent. Much as they may love the parent, there might be deep shame about being inadequately parented or being unable to induce enough love in the parent that they would be there for them in the way the Saver needed.

Some Savers grew up in environments where they felt powerless in their circumstances because of abuse, neglect, or deprivation that they tried to overcome by being helpful or saving in some way, or where one person's or a few people's help and support were pivotal to their survival. So they may not have been helped enough or did receive support or were even saved, and they're trying to make up for that. They may have seen, heard, and experienced things that no child—hell, no adult—should, and may feel disproportionate guilt for not being able to save or help someone, or a misguided culpability in their circumstances, or feel bad that they're okay where others aren't or didn't survive.

Some assessed the circumstances in their environment and identified that their role needed to be one of helping, such as dimming their light to let another family member shine, acting incompetent, or mediating between family members. It can even be that they got themselves into problems so that they gave another family member something to do. They may have felt passed over, resentful, underappreciated, and underacknowledged, but due to their given (or assumed) responsibility, have a strong sense of duty that makes them jump in and get involved in other people's boundaries and business.

No matter the grown-ups' intentions or struggles, when children grow up too soon or the adults emphasize selflessness and helpfulness, they learn to deny and sacrifice themselves. They're so oriented to other people's circumstances and struggles that they feel guilty about themselves, no matter how in strife they are, because of their enmeshed relationships. It becomes their job to try to be the external solution to other people's internal struggles or to be the salve to whatever's going on in their lives, and they lose the child in themselves as well as their *no* and their sense of their own and other people's boundaries in the process. Once they are aware of someone else's needs, real or projected, and their people pleaser is activated, they find it difficult to distinguish themselves from the other person and often feel as if helping others by sacrificing themselves is for the good of everyone even when those same people feel otherwise.

This really flares up when they experience challenges because in knowing what they have done for others, it doesn't seem "right" that they're now feeling unsafe. They feel disapproved of and neglected, and while all pleasers feel owed, the sentiment *after everything I've done for you* applies to Savers the most. While, for instance, Efforters put in a lot of effort, their efforts are about proving themselves, not applying their efforts for others to be helped. Savers feel rejected wholesale when, despite their help, they feel neglected or experience issues because it's taken as "this person disapproves of *what I have done for them*," and it's the *for them* bit that leaves them feeling wounded, used, or abused.

Given what they've internalized about what it takes to be a good person or where their values lie, someone not liking them, taking issue, or not improving can make them feel as though they've failed. At the same time, people no longer needing them or improving "too much" can also trigger a sense of rejection, especially if the person isn't showing the gratitude that the Saver pretends they're not looking for.

In using saving to meet their needs, when they've tolerated too much and let it pass or they feel as if they've been and done more than enough, they can erupt and also expect the other person not to take issue with it. In fact, sometimes they will allow themselves to get to the point of urgency and desperation so that they can leverage their anger as a justification for why the person should do as they want. When accused of being controlling or manipulative, or someone points out that their good intentions are harmful, the Saver may feel genuinely confused or very triggered and defensive. They also, however, sometimes fear people getting better or changing or only want them to improve if they get to benefit from it.

It infuriates the Saver and feels like rejection and abandonment when people won't change even though it would clearly be in their best interests, but they don't acknowledge that they want the person to change in ways that would make the Saver feel better.

Savers take a back seat to put other people's problems front and center. They act needless or low-maintenance while hiding their agenda and needs behind the veneer of their generosity, and are significantly affected by overgiving and over-responsibility. As they learned to derive their value from giving of themselves through help and sacrifice, they gravitate to relationships and situations that reflect that same dynamic or that allow them to play their role, which means that they're only really "at home" where there's a problem. Of course, by sacrificing themselves, they wind up feeling resentful, neglected, burdened, and subsumed.

Consciously or not, saving is their way of hiding while pretending they aren't. Sure, they're trying to be there for others, but it's because they're attempting to right the wrongs of the past where they couldn't help and save or where they didn't get what they needed, and so they're ultimately trying to save themselves.

YOU KNOW YOUR STYLE IS SAVING IF . . .

- Your primary means of feeling good about yourself and pleasing others is being needed and involved in other people's problems through helping, rescuing, and taking on their responsibilities.
- You don't say no because you're over-responsible; you think it will hurt, abandon, or inconvenience the other party; you don't want to look like a Bad Person; or you're afraid of being made redundant and their needing someone else.

- When life doesn't go your way; people anger, reject, or disappoint you; or you don't receive validation and recognition, you respond by thinking about all the sacrifices you've made, how you were "just trying to help" and your good intentions, and feeling not good enough, replaceable, underappreciated, taken advantage of or abused, or that you always come last.
- You tell people what you think they want to hear (and sometimes what *you* want them to hear) because you want to think it will help or save them or give them a boost, or because it makes you feel good about yourself.
- You have a strong sense of feeling obligated and guilty, so you feel as if it's your duty to help or fulfill someone's needs or wants even if it's to the detriment of their and your well-being and the health of the relationship.
- You, on some level, believe that being a good person who helps and the amount of effort you put into trying to make other people's lives better or save them from themselves means that people should appreciate you and not abandon you.

As a Saver, especially if you have gooding traits, you possibly were aware of your people-pleaser ways but might feel very uncomfortable with this notion of having a hidden agenda or saving yourself. But helping, supporting, and giving to people isn't merely something you do; it's your identity. It's important for you to be perceived this way in order to feel accepted and safe.

A combination of seeking a sense of self through feeling good about being there for others or sacrificing yourself to be there for others, saving relies heavily on *should*s, obligations, emotional blackmail, and fear of having too much of a self that might cause alienation or abandonment. As a result, it prioritizes being and looking good by signaling good intentions or sacrificing yourself unnecessarily, even when it means feeling like you're nobody if you're not doing things for others.

When you struggle to or don't say no, it's because you believe it's your duty to say yes; otherwise you feel as though you're hurting the person or leaving them in the lurch. In feeling needed, you fear they won't be able to manage, that the problem won't be solved without you, or that you won't survive and will be made redundant for saying no on that occasion. Because it's all about appearing and being good and helpful through selflessness, *no* feels like selfishness and a violation of an ethical code.

Rather than being involved in people's lives and problems from a place of being yourself and letting that dictate what you say yes and no to, you take on the persona of a self-sacrificer, willing to drop everything, including yourself, and supposedly without expecting anything in return. You may be a lifelong Saver who, whether it's through gooding or efforting traits, has derived a level of purpose and value or wanted to help and save, but lack the validation, recognition, relationship, or experience that you feel, on some level, would make you feel whole.

Needing to be needed is the crux of your challenges because it creates a hidden agenda. The identity of saving seems so altruistic, well-intentioned, and focused on other people's best interests that it's unexpected that you might want something back. By focusing on the image, you pretend that you don't have needs or an agenda or that things don't bother you, not realizing how this makes you inadvertently disingenuous. Whether it's needing your virtue to be seen or sacrificing yourself with effort, you haven't copped on to the fact that even if you're giving, there are wrong reasons. And so you can be blind, not only to where you're hurting yourself and going way past your limits, but also where you're enabling somebody or meddling.

Gaby felt put-upon and taken advantage of by her family but felt too guilty to say no. Recognizing not only how her actions had given her a sense of control that helped her feel less scared of owning her life but also that she was in a vicious cycle of enabling the very behavior she said she didn't like allowed her to see how she was colluding in the problem. Like many pleasers, she was driven by proving or getting something . . . that she already had. Clearly, she had more than proved her helpfulness.

Of course helping and supporting and, where appropriate, saving someone are good things, but they need to be done with boundaries, otherwise we turn people into problems to exercise our emotional baggage and ego on. That's why there's a shift in how charity workers approach aid because when you keep seeing people as a problem, you can wind up dehumanizing the very people you want to help.[1]

It may be a shock to realize that you're not as selfless as you think, but this is a good thing because this pretense is killing your spirit and possibly burning you out. But—and here's where the rubber hits the road— sacrificing isn't the same as *giving*, and if you're always the one giving or saving, then everyone else has to be taking or victimizing themselves, and that's shitty boundaries that don't serve anyone.

Those feelings and needs you pretend you don't have and the belief that people haven't appreciated "everything you've done" are letting you know that you need to listen to and take care of yourself. Your saving is a double standard of acting like you have no needs while elevating or even exaggerating other people's needs and making yourself responsible for them while being under-responsible for yourself. The persona of "strength" means that you don't let people in and act as if they're the only ones who can have problems until you've burned yourself out, but you're giving away something you don't give to yourself while also expecting others to do for you what you won't do for yourself.

On some level, you reason that you're always going to give way more than others or that you have already done so much across your life that you're almost beyond reproach or that it shouldn't be that hard for the other person to reciprocate even a little.

But you're trying to gain happiness without being seen, without truly giving of yourself in the sense of being boundaried and allowing yourself to be a full person. You pretend that you don't know what's going on and how you're not so effected, but you matter too, and that's not something you need to earn. People don't know how much you emotionally black-mail yourself into doing stuff, and ultimately, if you don't feel genuinely good after you help, it's not help: It's an agenda.

COMMON THEMES

- Being partial to fixer-upper and rehabbing relationships where you believe that your presence alone lifts their spirits, or you make yourself so indispensable or make such a positive difference to their life that the person should stay and not abandon you because they, in theory, don't have a reason to leave.
- Having a fear of inconveniencing others if you think it's going to result in their perceiving you negatively or their not needing you, or your not feeling in charge.
- Being enmeshed with your family and so finding yourself at their beck and call or immersed in their dramas, which sometimes results in neglecting your responsibilities and commitments.
- Priding yourself on being sympathetic and empathetic, and perhaps describing yourself as an empath and thinking it's wrong not to help if you can.
- Perhaps avoiding intimate relationships with friends or romantic partners because of worry about how it might interfere with rescuing if they are more emotionally secure and boundaried and so query your enabling behavior.
- Making yourself indispensable/helpful to people you don't get on with so that you don't displease them (or look or feel like a Bad Person) by confronting what you dislike or feel uncomfortable about.
- Excusing people even when you outright know that they have been up to shadiness and giving people a hundredth "second chance" to avoid accepting the truth.
- Acting like an emotional airbag in your romantic relationships, so you provide a soft landing when they're fresh out of a breakup by being the rebound, or soaking up all their feelings, or cushioning them from

having to face their responsibilities, whether to themselves or the relationship, by taking on the lion's share.

- Foisting money or possessions on romantic partners and friends even though they haven't asked and then looking for payback when the relationship sours.

- Being expected to be the one to manage things when an elder relative becomes ill or has additional needs because your other family members disappear or assume that you're the most responsible one or you're "good" at sorting things out.

STRENGTHS *AND* CHALLENGES

- Being good at connecting people, mediating, and spotting and solving problems also means possibly getting caught up in other people's business and feeling overly responsible for a solution, or focusing too much on finding another problem, even when people want to move on.

- Being the go-to person when people are in need, possibly in every area of your life, because you seem so capable, empathetic, supportive, solutions-oriented, and so forth, leaving you caught between feeling needed, valued, and purposeful, and pigeonholed, put-upon, mistreated, but afraid of not being needed.

- Being very resilient in the sense that you can get the job done, tolerating a lot, and throwing yourself into being there for others, but being overreliant on this identity of strength means that you don't ask for help and have a fear of appearing weak while also expecting people to realize that you're drowning and step in, but then still struggling to accept help even when it's obvious you need it.

THINGS TO WATCH OUT FOR

- Burnout and illness, including chronic illness, from being of service, stopping you in your tracks. *I'm so nice . . . I'm just trying to be helpful . . .*

I just wanted to help . . . They need my help/support . . . I don't understand why they come to me and then don't bother to follow my advice . . . I'm exhausted . . . Why does everyone come to me?

- When you feel people pulling away from you, manipulating the situation to try to get them to come back even if they really need to jog along, and so perhaps switching from pretending to be need free to suddenly being a live wire of needs and acting like you can't manage without them.

- Centering your feelings, good intentions, and deeds when people point out where you've erred or harmed them instead of acknowledging the impact of your actions.

- Putting people on pedestals, whether it's yourself or others. Aside from this being like worshipping false idols, whoever isn't on the pedestal feels beneath the other.

THE JOY OF SAYING NO: QUICK SHIFT

- If, no matter what you do, nothing or very little changes in a relationship or situation, or even if things appear to shift for a while, they return to the status quo, it's because you're taking responsibility for a problem that's not yours. Trying to be the solution to someone else's problem never works because it stops them from learning a lesson they need to learn and makes you over-responsible for them while being under-responsible for yourself. No matter how well-intentioned you consider yourself to be, no matter how much you perceive them to be struggling, you need to be boundaried and take your own agenda out of it, otherwise, you're not really *giving*.

- Check in with the reasoning for your style of helping and rescuing. Yes, there's a fear of failure or what might happen with the person, but think about what's been happening and whether the specific things you've done are helping this person, but also what problems it might be causing, not only for you but for them.

- If you can help or be involved only if it's on your terms or if you get something in return, pause. When feeling comfortable in this relationship relies on your sticking to a certain role, this is a sign that you are in a pattern, not really helping and giving in the fullest sense. How could you be of help and support without your seeing it as your *job* in the relationship or having an expectation of what the person should be and do in return?

7

SUFFERING

In the years since their divorce, Mariama's ex trashed her at every opportunity even though he'd opted not to be actively involved in their children's lives with consistent visitation or paying child support. Despite being urged to go down the legal route to protect herself and the children and put some much-needed boundaries around the situation, she resisted because she didn't want the kids to think that she was the type of mother who'd stopped them from having a relationship with their father. She thought being a Good Mother and not chasing him for child support or limiting how much he could abuse her would make him "be nice" and stop the abuse.

Instead, he upped his campaign of harassment and abuse, with it culminating in a terrifying altercation in front of their children. It was only when he refused to acknowledge their distress and the impact of the ordeal, including their PTSD, that she finally drew the line. For a little while.

But even after limiting access, Mariama still held out hope of him having his come-to-Jesus moment in which he registered all her good deeds, apologized, and made things right. She felt resentful of having to create the overdue boundaries and that it was unfair given that she hadn't done anything wrong. She thought that suffering was how you make people stop and change their ways and that it shows how much of a Good Person you are, not realizing that it kept her superglued to situations that hurt her and her children.

> Suffering is using self-dislike and consciously and unconsciously putting one's self in a position of hardship, distress, and frustration to be "good," to influence and control other people's feelings and behavior, and to call attention to a need.

The primary driver and motivation for suffering is, ironically, using being the best of the worst to feel secure and worthy and so *needing to suffer*. While Sufferers may have always been in this style, it can also be a suffering version of the other styles where the person has gone too far and fallen on their sword. They keep trying to show how good they are to try to get a person to acknowledge, appreciate, or love them the way that they want, even though they expose themselves to further harm and extend their torment.

Pleasers who feel as if they always get the shitty end of the stick and that they're routinely picked on or misunderstood will recognize themselves in this style and the following roles:

The Scapegoat	The Troublemaker/Rebel
The Weak One	The Messed-Up One
The One Who Mustn't Succeed	The Truth Teller
The Problem Child	The Outsider/Black Sheep

THE ORIGINS OF SUFFERING

Sufferers often grew up in an environment where there was this notion that suffering is what makes you a good or better person, or where people were treated like problems or their issues were ignored or downplayed no matter how acute or real. Talking positively about one's self or their accomplishments may have been regarded as boastful, narcissistic, or getting ideas above one's station. An adult may have martyred themselves or tolerated mistreatment from their spouse or even their children, modeling this attitude of enduring not only being taken advantage of or abused but also self-neglect.

They learn to build an identity that essentially makes them the Best at Being the Worst. It's making themselves feel "special" albeit in a negative way. They received attention for letting people take out their problems on them, taking a back seat, or for continuing to take what someone was meting out without showing that they were bothered.

Some arrived at playing this role because they copied it from someone else. If the collective identity in the family was suffering, it can almost have felt, at times, as if they were trying to outdo one another on who had it harder. The Sufferer may have felt as if they had to not have things "too good" lest it alienate them from family members, and so victimizing themselves became their way of doing their part in the family.

It may have been that burning out, hustling, or even standing by your abusive partner was a badge of honor, so it was as if collapsing on the job or being maxed out by other people's problems or the relationship was something to achieve.

Some arrived at suffering because they were always the Problem, not because they actually were but because someone in the environment took out their problems on them or made them a proxy for their problems. And so the Sufferer, even though they hated being treated this way, conversely learned to derive value from being the Scapegoat, as it was how they were "needed," or they were afraid of being abandoned and having nowhere to go. It was their "job" to hide other people's responsibilities and shroud them in the illusion of whatever lie they were telling themselves. In a twisted way, they hoped for retribution and recognition one day where the person would acknowledge all the lies and how great the Sufferer is, but instead, that person might deny they're even scapegoating in the first place and make themselves the victim, all while continuing to scapegoat the Sufferer.

It may be that they were the target of a sibling who seemed to get away with murder, making the Sufferer's life hell but also creating a sense of isolation where it was everyone else clubbed together versus them. Maybe they weren't believed or their concerns were dismissed, especially if they were the eldest and supposed to be "setting an example." Their sibling may have been able to lie with impunity or even pin their "crimes" on the Sufferer, and it may have become clear that no matter how good they were, no matter how much effort they made, no matter how they helped or tried to avoid discomfort, they weren't pleasing anyone, and no one was going to take their side.

If all eyes were on someone else, maybe because that person had additional needs or maybe because they'd been appointed (or assumed to be) the Favorite, the Sufferer may have learned to play the role of Second Best or Last in Line but taken to, whether in childhood or later life, putting themselves in pain to try to finally get the support they need. After spending their childhood and part of adulthood believing they were this big-ass problem or a burden and then discovering that this isn't true, they're trying to get what they're owed, either by getting people to validate their experiences and acknowledge where they failed or by giving them new problems to make a better job of supporting them so that they can right the wrongs of the past.

It may have been that when they were sick or going through problems, it was the first time they'd finally had their parents' attention, or even that knowing their parent was worrying about them meant that at least they weren't focused, for instance, on another sibling. Sometimes it's that siblings competed with their problems to have the adults' attention and that the Sufferer went back and forth with them or that they gave up and stepped back, acting over-responsible and as if they had no needs, and then reverted back in adulthood.

In fact, they may have realized that the only way to feel connected to their family or to shift or hold attention is to have problems, and so, unconsciously, they don't get themselves together or they keep getting into shitty situations and relationships so that someone—for instance, their parent—has to step in and come to the rescue. This means that they can have a fear of not being in pain, of getting better, because then they'll lose the attention or they'll put the other person out of the job of their role. They might even feel as if moving forward is abandoning, for instance, their parent, and so might unconsciously relapse with an addiction so they don't have to grow up but also so that the parent doesn't feel redundant. The parent might, for instance, be a Saver, who doesn't realize that there's a pattern of enabling.

Sufferers also often learn their role from experiencing pain and trauma that wasn't recognized or supported, including possibly being called a hypochondriac, so they may have stayed in pain to try and call attention to the original neglect and finally get what they needed. There might be this sense of injustice that someone else was the Favorite or the Priority even though the Sufferer had bigger needs. This might feel particularly aggrieving if they experienced something traumatic and even then the other person still had the focus despite having lesser needs at that time. Even when the Sufferer was moving forward and achieving success in their own right, they may have felt the need to put the brakes on it and try to get people to acknowledge what they wouldn't in the past. It might be that family may have dismissed or turned a blind eye to abuse or closed rank when the Sufferer tried to get everyone to see what was going on, effectively causing them to become isolated from the group and feel abandoned. They might go back and forth with family, trying to get them to see it, including others who were also victims of it, only to feel invalidated all over again.

Even if they don't realize it, and even if they don't know what it's for, they're looking for redemption. They're trying to pay off guilt about *something*—for instance, being inadequately parented or experiencing traumatic events, even though these weren't their fault. They're also, however, trying to make people feel guilty. By absorbing the blame and pretending to be guilty, they try to create a tipping point with their suffering so that others will step up.

As Sufferers try to prove how good they are and earn their needs being met through being in pain, it can feel excruciating and deeply triggering when they come up against life's inevitables because it's felt as a rejection of their victimhood and their experiences. It's like, *Jeez, how much more do I have to feckin' bleed here?* There can be this sense of being braced for disappointment and getting hurt while conversely being surprised that someone doesn't like them or takes issue or isn't willing to accommodate their pain.

They are, like all pleasers, trying to earn the credits to limit or avoid anything that makes them feel unsafe, but are also caught between wanting relief from hurt but also using hurt to try to connect and be taken care of. When things don't go their way or they feel under-supported and neglected, all the unacknowledged pain erupts again and it's like, *After everything I've suffered, you have the audacity to treat me this way and still won't accept me!*, prompting not only deep pain, but also rage at the lack of acknowledgment. They feel that given everything they've been through, people should make accommodations for them and hold back on things like criticism.

They find it hard to understand why someone doesn't like them, takes issue, or won't change in spite of their suffering, not realizing that the person might think they're disingenuous precisely because of their willingness to suffer. And people who get off on exploiting and hurting others will seize on this need to please via suffering.

Sufferers, when they've essentially used their boundaries as currency and let themselves be walked over, feel understandably used and abused, but also confused as to why someone either wouldn't want to make things right and stop behaving in this way or why they wouldn't want a relationship with someone who will take whatever's thrown at them. They think willingness to suffer is unconditional love. In reinforcing whatever role they learned in childhood by which they've defined themselves, rejection pokes at the lie that this is the only way for them to be. Rather than say no, they go along with the situation, let the violations stack up and the resentments mount, and then use this to justify exiting abruptly or erupting in anger.

This creates a sacrifice-resentment dynamic, which is also present with Savers, where Sufferers keep sacrificing and martyring themselves while feeling resentful at "having to" do so. They want the other person to change and reason that it would be for the person's benefit, not recognizing it's really for themselves.

Sufferers are waiting to be rescued, and when it doesn't happen, they hurt some more in an effort to make rescue more likely. They think that they have to earn happiness and prove goodness through suffering and that there's a magic amount of suffering that will suddenly make everything in life go right. Instead, they're setting themselves up for more pain, not realizing that by deriving an identity from suffering, they feel as if they have to stay that way, rendering them powerless and helpless when they don't have to be.

YOU KNOW YOUR STYLE IS SUFFERING IF . . .

- Your primary means of trying to gain self-worth, please others, and get them to meet your needs, desires, and expectations is trying to prove how good and deserving you are by being in pain and need.
- You don't say no because you think you have no choice but to put up with something, you don't feel as if you've earned the right to say it yet, you're afraid that people will go away and that they will never meet your needs, or you're secretly afraid of having to take responsibility for yourself.
- When life doesn't go your way; people anger, reject, or disappoint you; or you don't receive validation and recognition, you think about everything you've let slide, the chances you've given them to stop doing the

things that hurt you, everything you've endured to prove how good or loving you are (or how you're not what they say you are), fear that they're going to convince people of your badness or unworthiness, or how it's your fault and you're unlucky or never good enough.

- You tell people what you think they want they want to hear (and sometimes what *you* want them to hear) because you hope that they will feel guilty and obliged to reciprocate and meet your needs, wants, and expectations.

- You have a strong sense of feeling obligated and guilty, so you feel as if it's your duty to suffer to make someone else feel good about themselves or to stay stuck in your pattern so that it doesn't disrupt the status quo of the relationship or your family's dynamic.

- You believe that suffering is a sign of how good you are and that eventually it's going to pay off and you're finally going to get the validation and recognition you've been chasing.

This style of pleasing is often the least obvious because you and even people around you don't register how this is about keeping a painful dynamic in play that everyone is invested in to some degree. It's also that, given how much pain you're in and why, you don't feel as if you're pleasing anyone. But, on some level, you feel that you have to be this way for someone and that if you stopped, it would be a problem.

Your sense of self is derived from being the victim and struggling. That doesn't mean that you haven't been a victim, but how you perceive yourself and what you expect of others and the world is through this lens that you're a hurtable person or that you've been flattened too much by what you've already endured. Suffering relies heavily on a sense of enmeshment, *should*s, and taking the fall, and so it puts being in pain and taking the blame above all else, creating more pain.

When you struggle to say no or don't say no, it's because it contradicts your victim identity. You feel as if you have no choice in things and don't want to give people Yet Another Bloody Reason to have a problem with or hurt you, so you get to feel hard done by, victimized, and powerless.

There's a fatigue with *no*, but also, if you're not pissed off about something or feeling victimized, then you're no longer in the role or other people aren't in theirs.

Because of what you've been through and feeling repeatedly invalidated or that you're valid and supported only if you're in distress, the idea of being yourself feels complicated, not least because you're not sure who you are without these problems or having another drama on the horizon. You may have learned to derive a level of acceptance and security from this position and don't want to disrupt the status quo, especially with family who may rely on this role even if no one's admitting it, but given how much you've suffered, it's like, *I've started so I must finish,* and you're gonna ride this donkey until it collapses. Your suffering might follow a similar pattern (e.g., torrid romantic relationships, same argument with family) while other areas of your life might be good, or it might be a free-for-all where there's drama popping off in every area or it feels as if you slide from one thing to another.

Feeling as if you need to suffer is the root of your pain. We humans have a broad spectrum of needs, but suffering isn't one of them. The suffering, though, is the cover for other needs that you veer between denying and revealing. Suffering is how you connect and how you try to get attention, affection, and more, and this means it's as if you don't really feel you can do or be something without having to feel like shit about it to a degree. You try to influence and control other people's feelings and behavior by sacrificing yourself, but it opens you up to more suffering. When you have a mentality that struggle and pain are proof of effort and goodness, you will not allow yourself to be in situations that are not painful. You unwittingly, and sometimes deliberately, put yourself in harm's way or force yourself to suffer.

This is what we see with Mariama, who had the means to shut down her ex, but that would have meant not having the identity of still being wronged by him. She hadn't realized that she was acting as if she were a participant in the Suffering Olympics in which proving how good she is with how much she hurts will eventually be rewarded. Yes, her ex's behavior was shady, abusive, and unfair, but by holding on to her suffering role to try to make a point to him, she was missing the point that she needed to create boundaries for her children's and her own well-being.

Humans experience pain, problems, and trauma, and they do suffer for a time, and yes, sometimes by no doing of their own, they suffer needlessly because of what others withhold despite having the power to make right the situation, like what we see with poverty, hunger, or access to health care. Suffering, though, isn't something to use as a badge of honor or a claim for what you think you're owed while not recognizing what you're also doing to yourself. You cover up your agenda with being nice and being the one to suffer, but don't realize where you want the person to stop hurting you so that you can feel better without owning what you're doing it to yourself by blocking yourself from having boundaries.

You have been through a lot, and there is no denying that, but the irony is your suffering is denying it because the identity doesn't allow you to gain access to the support, resources, relationships, and things that differ from your identity, so your people pleasing extends your suffering. Although you may have some of these things, unconsciously, you're stopping yourself from getting "too much" because that doesn't fit your identity. It's also why you might self-sabotage when healthier situations or people present themselves because it doesn't match your feelings of worthiness.

What you're doing doesn't feel good, and no one is entitled to your "pleasing" them in this way. Suffering is this fairy tale where the Good Sufferer endures pain in a gamble in which you lose now to win big later, but you're losing even more of yourself. Boundaries, which you often see as punishment and guilt inducing, are the very thing that will liberate and protect you.

COMMON THEMES

- Typical thoughts like, *I have to go last. I'm unlucky. It's my fault. People are out to screw me. I have no choice but to put up with this. I love too hard.*

This is as good as it gets. I only did what they wanted. Let someone else have the limelight; maybe they'll give it to me one day.

- Bracing for being hurt so you don't allow yourself to enjoy things too much or feel too disappointed if it goes wrong, and blaming things going awry on relaxing too much.

- Posting tumultuous life events on social media to drop hints about your suffering, possibly worrying loved ones who then reach out.

- Feeling aggrieved by someone, and then almost campaigning for people to take your side, even if it's not necessary, in a very *you're either with me or against me* mentality.

- Fearing, on some level, that if you allow yourself to heal, grow, and learn "too much," then the people who've hurt you won't see their wrongdoings or might even take credit for your progress.

- Staying connected to exes or other people you don't want to be around who will exploit you for favors or ego stroking because you're keeping them sweet so they don't hurt you (or so that they don't spontaneously combust into a better person when you're not around to benefit from it).

- Believing that "pain is love" and thinking there must be something inherently good about someone who would hurt themselves in an attempt to love others, and so unwittingly being drawn to painful relationships where you feel like the more you hurt, the more it means you're in love.

- Casting people in the role of Savior/Fixer/Helper/Healer and then feeling resentful when they treat you like a victim, take over, or don't live up to your expectations, and then they become the Problem.

- Assuming that everyone has it better than you so not seeing a loved one's struggles or even the impact of your actions because you're too caught up in your pain and your efforts.

- Avoiding being in relationships for several years at time, feel guarded, meeting someone who bulldozes your walls to gain your trust, only to get hurt by this intense and unhealthy relationship and recoil in confusion as to why you are hurt again. And lather, rinse, repeat.

STRENGTHS *AND* CHALLENGES

- You can seem very durable and resilient, won't complain about having a lot to do, and may enjoy the challenge of problem-solving and organizing, but may find it difficult to communicate when you don't have the bandwidth or when something isn't your responsibility.
- Even though it can be in stark contrast to suffering, you can be independent, self-sufficient, and reliant, but it can mean keeping people at a distance or becoming isolated.
- You will accept more help than most other pleasers *but* can then feel the need to feign incompetence or let yourself be someone's pet project to keep getting help or connection.

THINGS TO WATCH OUT FOR

- Allowing things to escalate to create urgent need. It's like when someone exaggerates an event because they don't think that the truth is enough on its own. Your need is enough on its own without exposing you to unnecessary pain.
- Not allowing yourself to learn from a past mistake or failure that you've likely exaggerated or distorted, and instead, holding yourself back, so you keep rubbing your face in it lest you relax, try again, and expose yourself to a bigger future pain.
- Seeing burnout as a badge of honor and so not feeling invested in identifying the root causes of it.
- Becoming obsessed when you feel as though you've been discarded and forgotten by someone you suffered a great deal for.

THE JOY OF SAYING NO:
QUICK SHIFT

- What if you're not the best or worst person and, instead, you are human? There are far better ways to feel good about yourself than trying to be superior by holding the Olympic gold medal for goodness achieved by suffering or exacerbating inferiority by giving yourself the grand prize for being the Best of the Worst. This doesn't mean you haven't been through things and that certain people haven't taken advantage or abused you, but these don't make you "the Best or the Worst"; they make you human.

- Ask yourself: Who am I without these problems? Sometimes some of the problems we have are part of our identities. They cater to the roles we're playing in our lives. Hence if we stop having the problem, we stop playing the role. If we derive identity, worthiness, and purposefulness from the role, though, that's the agenda behind our problems.
- Consider what it is that you always notice and value in people or what it is that tends to frustrate and upset you in your interpersonal relationships. This is telling you about what you *need*.

PART 3

THE SIX STEPS FOR FINDING THE JOY IN *NO*

The joy of saying no is about the joy that can and will follow when you become a more honest version of yourself by choosing preference over outdated programming. It's aligning with who you are and want to be, as well as how you want to feel and continue feeling and the relationships, opportunities, and activities that matter. It's about the impact, the true meaning and consequences of saying no, and how it opens you up to receiving a life that looks and feels more like yours. You get to be alive instead of telling big little lies and hiding out.

How do you get to feel, not just immediately after saying no but in the days, weeks, months, and years that follow?

How does *no* allow you to listen to your needs, expectations, desires, feelings, and opinions?

What are you saying no to?

> And what do you, as a result of allowing you to say no, allow
> yourself to say yes to? What becomes possible, and who do
> you get to become?

Despite your efforts to please everyone else to feel needed, worthy, and purposeful and to avoid discomfort and pain, you haven't found the joy in saying yes either because you haven't been saying no as much as you need and want to, so your *yes* hasn't been authentic and loving of yourself. You've been hurt, possibly a lot.

Sometimes you will hate how saying no feels, not because it or you are wrong but because you're finally feeling your feelings and recognizing how uncomfortable you are with vulnerability and the possibility of disappointing others. Your emotional baggage is showing itself. In that moment, you grieve the version of you that used to think that avoiding *no* was the Way. You release a little more of that fantasy, the old stories and judgments, and you're a little lighter because you're healing, growing, and learning.

It can be tempting to stay in your uncomfortable comfort zone because you figure that at least it's familiar and that it surely can't get any worse. Until it does. Whatever you're prepared to settle for is what you're going to get, and joy, peace, and contentment lie outside of your people-pleasing comfort zone.

Let go of pursuing instant gratification and gambling with your well-being in the hope of eventually being rewarded. You already have more than enough experience of saying yes inauthentically, even when well-intentioned and self-protective, to know that it causes more problems than it solves. People pleasing might relieve tension in the moment, but between how you wind up feeling afterward and the medium- to long-term hangover, it's time to stop trying to manage other people's feelings and behavior and honestly say no *and* yes to manage yours. It will take time, but you are worth the investment.

In these final chapters, I share the six steps for reclaiming yourself from the cycle of people pleasing. Doing all the steps is powerful, but doing even one will help break the pattern and inadvertently help you do the others. Let's set some realistic expectations from the outset:

Don't overcomplicate things. Whether it's thinking that you won't be able to be kind and loving toward yourself until you've shown that you can get saying no "right," imagining that reparenting and having boundaries is complicated, or expecting that you won't slip up at some point, these all delay owning your boundaries and experiencing more joy.

There is no blueprint. You will have to take steps and be vulnerable to the unfamiliarity of it all, and then learn and refine as you go. It means listening to yourself, paying attention, messing things up, getting back up, and trying again. Before you tell yourself that you can't do this or that you have no idea how to start, check yourself. You've been running around all over the place trying to please everyone else. Now you're going to turn much of that bandwidth toward yourself.

You don't have to make a big leap. This is not least because it might scare the bejaysus out of you and cause you to backtrack. Instead, set the intention to have a more boundaried, responsible relationship with yourself. Small steps every day add up. What you do some or all of the time matters more than what you do occasionally or rarely, so when you consistently show up with an attitude of wanting to have healthier boundaries, you will experience the cumulative effect of investing in yourself. You'll learn the self-care of figuring out what does and doesn't work for you as you go along.

I recommend that you record insights and observations from going through these steps in a journal, the notes app on your phone, whatever's easy and accessible, because aside from it allowing you to acknowledge progress—especially when you're being human and doubting yourself—it's also your personal encyclopedia of what does and doesn't work for you. One day, not too long from now, you'll realize that you didn't automatically go to do something that used to hurt. Maybe you'll notice that you don't dwell on something like you used to. Progress.

Let's get started.

8

GET TO KNOW
YOUR PLEASER

n autumn 2014, as the Ebola epidemic raged in her home country of Sierra Leone, we invited my mother-in-law to stay for what we assumed was a few weeks but turned out to be eight and a half months. I'd had no qualms about her visit because we got on brilliantly, but a few months in, I was walking on the eggshells of her unvoiced unhappiness with me. When I eventually heard her criticisms, first via my husband and then in the midst of a *Dynasty*-style, literal fur-coat-flying showdown between her and my mother, it triggered a woundedness and rage that consumed me on and off for over a year. And between initially exhausting myself trying to keep a pristine home and facing my feelings and behavior day after day in my journal, I got to know my pleaser in a way I hadn't before.

On reflection, I recognized that while I had enjoyed and valued my relationship with my mother-in-law, my rage was the signpost that somewhere along the way I'd become overinvested in *finally* being somebody's adored daughter, until I realized I wasn't. Being unable to escape the deeply uncomfortable situation or pretend to be okay forced me to examine my pleaser habit and my "why" more closely.

When people pleasers feel sufficiently pissed off, hurt, or burned-out that they'll forgo politeness or appearing cool to make their position known, or they begin to recognize that they have an issue with saying no, it's not uncommon for a flurry of *no* activity to begin. We might erupt and unleash or let off a volley of *no*s as if to make up for lost time, leaving us embarrassed or ashamed by our behavior. Or we feel confused by why people we've restrained our *no*s with don't all roll over and accept them straightaway so that we can skip off into the sunset to our happily ever after. Even if we initially feel energized by our newfound power to say no, we might backtrack when we feel as if it's backfired or that we're not experiencing the desired results, only to then feel frustrated when people inevitably overstep boundaries or with ourselves for not making it stick.

While it took falling out with my mother-in-law to examine my pleaser in new and deeper ways, it was looking at the content of my days and weeks during this time that offered answers and helped me to gradually move forward.

If we don't understand our pleaser habits, including when we're triggered into it and our "why," we'll keep being caught off guard by the autopilot of our habits. This is why the first step in breaking the cycle of people pleasing and finding your *no* is getting to know your pleaser because you can't change what you don't know, and until you know your *no*, you can't know your *yes*.

It's a simple yet powerful exercise and experiment comprised of two parts: For one week you're going to gather intel about how and where you spend your *yes*, *no*, and *maybe* so that you gain a clearer picture of what is and isn't working for you. And then the following week, you're going to use that intel to have a go at cutting your *yes* in half.

We each have our own brand of people pleasing, so this step is about answering the question, *How and where does people pleasing show itself in my life?*

WEEK 1: GATHER DATA

The objective of this week is building a picture of where you spend your bandwidth. When you're being and doing things that reflect who you are—your values and boundaries—these will energize you. And when you're not, they're draining. And even if you're technically doing things you want to do, if you do them with little regard for your well-being, these will also become draining. So, for example, you can be a mother or worker, but do you have to try to be the idealized versions of these that you've been sold through the media and patriarchy? You can exercise or party, but do you need to max out?

While there will always be things that you're not necessarily crazy about doing, but they're a prerequisite to getting to do other things or they help your home or job tick along, most of what you do needs to be consciously agreed to. You need to turn off autopilot and stop being at the mercy of whatever life throws at you.

Use whatever is as easy and accessible as possible to note your observations. Decide on the level of data you want to record. For example, you could mark off each time you say yes, no, and maybe with a tick in the relevant column or keeping a bulleted list. Over the course of the week, make a note of the following:

Where are you experiencing discomfort? Notice where it shows up in your body, which feelings you quickly try to shut down, and whether you're tense, anxious, irritated, and so on.

What energizes you, and what drains you?

Where did you automatically say yes?

What causes you to ruminate or be self-critical?

What are your sources of anxiety and worry?

Which calls and texts do you dread answering?

What causes you to feel overwhelmed?

Who tends to not only receive most of your *yes*es but also benefit from and expect you to always say yes even if it's to your detriment? These are your people-pleasing entourage, and they're whom you need to be particularly mindful of your *yes* with.

Some things to keep in mind:

- Try to get a general sense of your pattern so that you have a truer picture of your week. You don't have to try to get every last *yes*, *no*, and *maybe*—rein in that perfectionist—but gather as much data as possible from the start to the end of your day.
- You don't have to track each *yes*, *no*, and *maybe* as it happens. It might be that every hour or two you quickly reflect and update your list.
- You will need to go a bit slower than you usually do because you're noticing the content of your day. I'm talking seconds, not minutes or hours.
- Don't rely on memory alone to acknowledge your habit. If that worked, you wouldn't need to read this book!
- As this is an observational week, don't put yourself under pressure to start shaking things up. Obviously if you're in a position to say no, go ahead though!

Spend a few minutes each day reviewing the data, noting particular observations about the day. Bullet points will do, but paragraphs are more than welcome. Notice the themes in your week—for example, the types of asks or situations, your reasoning, people involved, the time of day. How you do something is how you do a lot of things. If you cut corners and delay meeting basic needs like going to the bathroom to push on with whatever you're doing, that's a metaphor for how you treat your other needs. You will see themes to your feelings, thoughts, actions, and choices.

Bandwidth shifts over the course of the day and week. So many people front-load their schedule by heavily committing at the start of the week, possibly because they've had a little bit of rest, and then lose their mojo as the reality of their commitments and needs kicks in. Within a day or two, they're wrecked and counting down to their next bit of free time, or they continue cramming more into their schedule and expecting to keep up. Become aware of patterns so that you can capitalize on your bandwidth and rest and take on less when you need to. By understanding how you live and work, you say yes, no, and maybe in a way that meets your needs instead of treating yourself like a machine.

GET TO KNOW YOUR PLEASER BY YOUR STYLE

Gooders, pay attention to situations where you automatically slot into playing expected roles where you try to look like a Good Person and where you talk yourself into doing something because of how you think it might be perceived if you don't.

Efforters, pay attention to where you automatically go into over-drive trying to give 100 percent and where you take on too much by saying yes first and then registering what's involved or your overcommitment afterward.

Avoiders, pay attention to where you automatically go along with things and, even if it feels vague, a sense that the other person will disapprove or be annoyed or upset if you said what you really think or feel.

Savers, pay attention to where you automatically assume responsibility or involvement and where you don't think something will be done or that people will manage without you.

Sufferers, pay attention to where you automatically assume that it will be a problem if you say no or express what you need or want and where you feel resigned, powerless, or helpless.

WEEK 2: START SAYING NO

This week is about testing out your *no* by attempting to cut your *yes* in half so that you can get a sense of where you can say no without the sky falling down, and also notice who and what triggers anxiety and resistance as well as why. You won't necessarily cut your *yes* by 50 percent, but by going through the process of identifying half and contemplating and attempting to say no, you will have a fuller picture of your pleaser habit. You might surprise yourself with what it turns out you can say no to but will also find the hot spots where you currently find it near impossible to say no.

Some quick tips before you start:

- You might be sick to death of your people pleasing and ready to torch your old way of living by cutting your *yes* by more than half. I also get that at the opposite end, the idea of even cutting your *yes* by 10 percent might flood you with anxiety. Please embrace the experiment of the step and use it as an opportunity to listen to and respect yourself more than you usually do—and learn from it when you don't.
- Set the intention to reduce *yes*, as it will prime you to notice opportunities.
- Unless you interact with only one person or it's one particular person maxing out your *yes*, don't direct all of your *no*s at them, as you may have targeted them because they seem "easier."
- Start small and build up. For instance, maybe you begin by choosing where to go for dinner or choosing a meeting time that suits you instead of saying you don't mind.
- It's unrealistic to expect *no* to feel comfortable or good straightaway when you have negative associations and it's unfamiliar territory. Give it time. Notice how the feelings about the *no* change over time as well as the real consequences of it. So if you said no on day one and then felt panicky, now that you're at day two or further on, what actually happened?

SAMPLE SCRIPTS FOR SAYING NO WITHOUT SAYING THE WORD *NO*

I don't have the bandwidth.

I can't take on anything else today.

I'm unavailable.

I can't make it.

I already have plans.

I'll need more time.

I'm not really into [Zumba/drinking alcohol/threesomes], but thanks for asking!

That's not going to work for me./That doesn't work for me.

Thank you for thinking of me, but I won't be able to attend/do this.

Thank you for asking, but I'm not doing [insert whatever they've requested] while [insert whatever you're doing] (e.g., "Thank you for asking, but I'm not doing work events while the kids are on holiday.")

Here's what will work for me.

Let me tell you what I can do.

I'm already working on [task/project] which still has X minutes/hours/days/weeks to go. Do you want me to continue or shelve it for [the new task/project]?

NOTICE . . .

- Where you say no and it's fine or nothing "bad" happens.
- Where you feel the need to tell a big ol' story to justify saying no.

- Where you say no but then feel tempted to go back and say yes so that you don't have to deal with the tension.
- Where you shame yourself for saying no.
- Where you feel relieved.
- Who almost took it as a foregone conclusion that you would say yes and whether they were pissed off with you for saying no.
- Where you worry and about what.

No matter how small you consider the *no* to be, make sure you acknowledge and appreciate it because it's progress and bigger than you think. Building the habit of saying no comes from also saying it in those little ways that add up.

If you don't say no where you hoped you would, it's okay! Everything in its time. There will be another opportunity. Note the feelings, thought process, or circumstances around it so that you know what you're working with and can become more mindfully aware.

ACKNOWLEDGE YOUR ANXIETY

People pleasing is code for *I am/was anxious about* something. When you realize that your inner pleaser is present or you recognize it with the benefit of hindsight, acknowledge what it is you are or were anxious about: For example, *I am anxious that I won't be liked. I am anxious about letting people down. I am anxious that the person will hurt me or that I'll get into trouble.*

Taking the time to acknowledge this not only gives you the opportunity to take care of yourself by tapping into what you authentically need, want, expect, feel, or think in that instance, but it also stops you from tricking yourself into believing that your feelings, the answer you're tempted to give, or the thing you are about to do or have already done is about "pleasing" that person or doing what's right for the situation or the relationship. Remember, behind that anxiety is not only a part of you that wants to control the uncontrollable in some way but old anger about something, so being more mindfully aware allows you to process buried anger instead of reinforcing it.

When I feel particularly anxious and unsettled after saying no, I ground myself by opening my front door or looking out the window. Inside, it feels as if you pushed the detonator and Armageddon happened. In reality, when you see that the world isn't up in flames, you realize that you're okay.

AFTER THE TWO-WEEK EXPERIMENT

Now you will have greater awareness and knowledge of how you spend your bandwidth and where you need to say no, as well as your "why" and the tangible impact of your *yes* on your emotional, mental, physical, and spiritual well-being. You can see the relationship between how you spend your time, energy, and effort and how that impacts you emotionally, but you also see how the way you feel impacts how much energy and effort you can put in and how you need to spend your time.

Conducting this experiment isn't about trying to say no for a week and then going back to whatever you were doing beforehand or hoping that *no* will take hold without your having to get too uncomfortable. It's the first step in reclaiming yourself by becoming a recovering people pleaser, someone who recognizes they've had the habit but is committed to getting to know it and themselves so that they can break the pattern.

Take your time, and don't pressure yourself to "fix your life" in a fortnight because you sure as hell didn't get to this point in that amount of time. That doesn't mean it will take as long as you've had this habit to start breaking it—it won't—but trying to speed things up is another form of taking shortcuts and avoiding vulnerability, and that's how you got here in the first place. This is also about taking a holistic approach where instead of treating you or your life like a problem to be fixed, you use your greater understanding of your bandwidth to honor who you are and want to be; the things, relationships, and goals that matter to you; and the way that you want to feel and continue feeling.

This is a journey. You are still going to people-please sometimes. Hell, I know I do. But you will do it less and learn from those times when you do. You discover who you are by discovering who you're not, so use this data to practice discernment. In giving yourself the opportunity to recognize and learn how and where to invest your good qualities, time, energy, effort, and emotions in the right people and situations by being more intentional and authentic, you treat yourself like a worthwhile and valuable person. You will also come face-to-face with your baggage, and that's what we're going to delve into in the next step.

EMBRACING HEALTHY BOUNDARIES

- What you say no to defines what you can say yes to. Great relationships, jobs and opportunities, sense of self, and joyful feelings don't fit into shitty boundaries, so rather than judging yourself (or others for that matter) for having a bandwidth and needing to be discerning, see it as permission to breathe out and be more you.
- Bandwidth is personal, and you don't have the same bandwidth every day because your personal circumstances, including quality of sleep, how your body works, self-care, stress, and so forth, impact your capacity, so get to know yours.
- Don't compare your bandwidth to others who appear to do "more" or be Teflon-coated because you don't know the toll of their choices.
- It can be frustrating when circumstances, your personal conditions, impact your bandwidth and even make you feel that you are missing out and that your options are curtailed. But if you don't listen to your body and learn to respect whatever is going on with it and your life, you will only have less bandwidth due to exacerbating whatever's going on. If you stop going against yourself, it's amazing how much more bandwidth opens up because you are also more discerning.

- If you know that certain things sap your bandwidth even if you enjoy them, make room in your schedule, plans, and expectations for this. For example, if I have an event, I know I need to have a calmer week, including a couple of quieter days following the event.
- While, sometimes, saying no solves something 100 percent, sometimes it's a start that gives you breathing room to decipher your other *no*s or figure out what you do want to say yes to.
- You won't always be able to do everything you imagine you're supposed to do. Keep a "What I Did Today" list, especially if you tend to be unrealistic about how much time you have or how long things take.

TROUBLESHOOTING *NO*

Natalie, I don't have any time. What's the bare minimum I can do?

- Pick one thing you do daily (or that you do automatically when it presents itself) that represents your delaying your own need—emptying the dishwasher or tidying and cleaning instead of working on your passion project, for example. Just focus on that by slowing down a little to notice what you feel, think, or do. Ask yourself, *Why am I doing this? Do I have to do this right now or in this way?* How you do something is how you do a lot of things. Pick an aspect of it that you will do differently and experiment with that for a week or so. Learning to walk past the washing up and leave it until after I've done what I need to do or for someone else to do it has been quite an eye-opener.
- Which *yes* stayed on your mind despite it happening hours or even days ago? What is this telling you about the *no* you need to give next time or where you need to be more boundaried?

We live in a world where we're all busier than a CEO, but if you're still too busy to try either suggestion, get honest about why you've designed your life in such a way that leaves you feeling you have no time.

What about stuff I've already agreed to that's on the calendar that I can't (or don't want to) change?

You are the steward of your bandwidth. This isn't about saying no to things you want or genuinely need to say yes to. If you have commitments for next week and you legitimately can't change any of these, what else do you need to say no to in order to facilitate your showing up in a way that supports your well-being? It might be saying no to staying up late and saying yes to getting fresh air and making sure that you have meals and snacks, which means saying no to working or running around all day without taking a break. You might need to say, "Hey, I'm really stacked this week, so unless it's genuinely urgent, it will have to hold until next week, or you'll have to ask someone else." If you're that full and committed that you can't say no, don't take on any new *yes*es (to similar stuff) for that week and be mindful of how you schedule subsequent weeks rather than repeating the same schedule.

I feel overloaded and don't know where to start. Help!

As someone who used to be chronically overloaded and overscheduled with a never-ending to-do list, I hear you. Do you know what shook me up? Acknowledging that there's nothing on that list or in my schedule that I didn't put there whether through imposing it on myself or agreeing to it directly or through compliance or silence. I know, it sucks, and it's easy to say it's everyone else—lord knows I've sometimes resented my husband and kids for "giving" me so much to do—but you're the steward of your bandwidth. You've taken the all-important step of acknowledging your overwhelm—some people don't even realize this and think their normal is Energizer Bunny mode. Observe your schedule and to-do list without judgment and discern what is an actual must-do and what's coming from trying to fulfill or uphold an image. The brain doesn't differentiate between things you need or have to do versus wishful thinking and unnecessary tasks. So get it all out of your head onto paper and identify actual priorities. If everything's a priority, nothing is!

How do I know if I'm over my bandwidth?

The people-pleaser feelings communicate that you are saying yes for the wrong reasons and/or that you haven't been mindful of your own needs. You are "full" and way over your bandwidth. If very little energizes you, you are also over your bandwidth because you have spent too much of your bandwidth being drained and have nothing left.

I believe I should be able to do more and worry that I'm lazy. If I accept what I've learned about my bandwidth, I won't excel.

There's nothing wrong with having goals and aspirations, but the fact that you worry about "laziness" and you think you "should" be doing "more" points not only to your conditioning but also that you are pushing yourself to fulfill the idealized version of yourself and may have lost sight of a genuine "why" rooted in your values and boundaries. "Laziness" is a construct used to exploit, abuse, and dehumanize humans so that we comply, work harder, spend money, compete with one another, and don't question the dodgy system. Check yourself before you wreck yourself.

What if I'm a really busy person and it's part of my job (or role in the home) to solve other people's problems?

Of course, your job or business might involve being the go-to person, but make sure you're doing your actual job, meeting your priorities, and empowering others to solve their problems where possible. Are you creating unnecessary work for yourself through repetition, not delegating, or assuming that something is your responsibility when it isn't? If you're solving the same problems with the same people over and over again, then you're not solving the problem. How could you go about putting boundaries around your work so that everyone gets to flourish? If this is happening at home, check in with yourself about your expectations and *shoulds* and make sure you're not taking over in situations where the person could benefit or would even like to be able to figure it out themselves.

I've been through a difficult time and have tried to get back to normal but am struggling to do what I did before. What's wrong with me?

Nothing's "wrong" with you. You don't have the same bandwidth as before, and you were possibly already over your bandwidth. That doesn't mean that you will be at this level of bandwidth forevermore, but you need to acknowledge what you and your body need. If, for instance, you're unwell, have been through a loss, are dealing with a big change or several—so many of us had this with the pandemic—you cannot expect your bandwidth to be the same as usual. You will need to adjust rather than behaving like a machine, which means you will need to figure out what requires *no*. It doesn't mean you need to quit your job, but you need to identify where you've overspent on *yes*es or where, for the foreseeable future, you need to hit pause on some old expectations.

It's easier to say no at work when you're self-employed or you have no dependents. What about when you work with or for people where *no* is frowned upon?

Is it that you genuinely work with or for people who have zero tolerance for *no*? Or, is it that you don't say no anyway? Be honest with yourself. I'm self-employed, and I was the worst boss I ever had because I didn't know my limits and tried to please everyone, and my ego caused me to demand too much of myself. Dependents or no dependents, I—and many others, I might add—struggled to say no, so it's not really the people or the situation, although some will exacerbate it. It's how you feel about *no*. If you're working somewhere that prohibits *no*, you will need to move on in the medium- to long-term because otherwise you will break yourself.

Should I confront my people-pleasing entourage or cut them off?

No. When we realize who's benefited, we may feel taken advantage of and abused. But confronting or cutting off without cleaning up your side of the street by being more authentic with your *yes* and learning to say no is avoiding responsibility. Acknowledging what you hoped they'd do in return or who you hoped they'd become or even what you didn't have to deal with while they were around helps you step back a bit and own your part without owning theirs. "Confront" suggests you're presenting them with wrongdoing with the aim of getting them to own it or apologize. Sure, you can communicate that how things have been no longer works, how you're going to change, and what, if anything, you need them to do, but you can also show and tell through demonstrating it with your *no*. Don't get me wrong: If someone is an unhealthy influence in your life and the relationship cannot exist if you have healthier boundaries, getting some distance or removing them from your life may well be part of your boundaries.

9

RECOGNIZE YOUR BAGGAGE

When I look back on the fallout with my mother-in-law, it's plain as day to me that my complex relationship with my mother and the unconscious ways I'd learned to ward off criticism played a significant role in how I interacted with my mother-in-law and the sense of injustice and betrayal that I felt in the aftermath. And those same feelings reminded me of a multitude of experiences that, until we clashed, I didn't know still had a hold over me.

If you don't unearth the motivations for why you continue to think, feel, and do certain things that cause you pain and remove or curtail your options, you cannot have a choice in how you react. You don't know why you are reacting.

Whatever the specifics of your "why" that you began to uncover in the first step, the reason you say yes and avoid *no* in the way that you do is because of your emotional baggage. Understanding what drives your "why," the baggage behind it, is pivotal because then you can use being even a little bit more boundaried to break the cycle of people pleasing and allow yourself to evolve into being more you.

This powerful step teaches you to start taking responsibility, be more mindful, and not take other people's baggage so personally by using recognition of your own emotional baggage as an opportunity to create a better boundary in the present.

IN ANY GIVEN situation where you become anxious, fearful, guilty, irritated, overwhelmed, or any of the other people-pleaser feelings, or you say yes inauthentically, or someone triggers you, it's not that the person or situation isn't annoying, upsetting, hurtful, or whatever, but you wouldn't respond in the way that you do if it wasn't for your emotional baggage. While undoubtedly people get on your nerves, mistake your kindness for weakness, push your buttons, and hurt and disappoint you, how you respond in that moment and in the aftermath—especially when your response is automatic or leaves you feeling bad about yourself or stuck—is your baggage showing up. When you realize that you've been people pleasing because you recognize the actions, thinking, feelings, or undesirable outcome, and you've sufficiently calmed enough to be even a little self-reflective, it's time to ask: *What's the baggage behind it?*

- Whom and what does this person or situation remind you of?
- Where else have you felt, thought, and acted similarly?
- Where did you learn to respond in this way? Or, who taught you this response?

Each time you ask these questions, you access intel from your mental filing system (your subconscious) and nervous system. It's possible that what comes to mind will reflect a similar situation, but it's also possible that something you perceive to be "irrelevant" or "nonsensical" comes up. It isn't. Whatever springs to mind is a clue to what's going on because it's what your subconscious associates with the event. You're allowing yourself to evaluate why you do things in the way that you've done them for as long as you have and to decide if that's the response you want to proceed with. You now have an opportunity to not only recognize your past but pull yourself out of it into the present so that you can have an adult, boundaried response.

Remember, patterns occur when you're living unconsciously, so by getting off autopilot and allowing yourself to connect with the present instead of behaving as if you are in the past, you interrupt those patterns and start to shift and wake up. Doing so breaks down old patterns and updates your mental filing system.

In asking the question and recognizing and acknowledging that you do have baggage influencing your responses, you practice healthier boundaries. You distinguish between your thoughts, feelings, behavior, choices, body, and "stuff" versus someone else's, and in doing so, you also recognize and acknowledge that other people have baggage behind their responses too.

Speaking of other people's baggage, you can also use the question to recognize and consider the existence of other people's baggage. This doesn't mean psychoanalyzing them or overempathizing and deciding that because you know they've experienced X that you now need to not have a boundary. It's acknowledging in that moment where they don't respect boundaries or they struggle with themselves or something, that it's *their* thoughts, feelings, behavior, and choices reflecting *their* habits and *their* baggage. Rather than making it about you and how "pleasing" you have or haven't been, recognize their baggage. Humanize them. And then create a healthier boundary. In acknowledging mine *and* my mother-in-law's baggage, I stopped taking it so personally, and we're now in a far better, *boundaried* place.

The more your boundaries reflect the actual present, the more secure you begin to feel, the more your habitual emotional responses calm, and you start to feel like someone you can rely on, and you can sense more of your boundaries and honor them.

IMAGINE HOLDING ON to everything we've ever owned since birth, including the packaging and any residue. It would be an overwhelming hot mess. Even if we believe we've had very little or that we're not a heavy consumer, we've let go of things that no longer fit or work for us, simply by having outgrown them or finding something that does the job better or quicker. Our tastes, needs, and wants have changed over the years, and what we have (or no longer have) reflects who we've been, who we think we are, and who we'd like to be. It's why plenty of us have clothes we hope to fit in when we lose a few pounds, home improvement items gathering dust, or exercise equipment we plan to use but don't. It's why we have things that maybe make no sense to someone else but that we hold on to for sentimental value.

Despite becoming increasingly aware of the impact of our epic levels of consumption on our well-being, homes, other humans, and the planet and our need to be more conscious consumers, we haven't gotten the memo and applied this to our emotional baggage. This emotional residue created by the old stories, judgments, habits, misunderstandings, and feelings from past events impacts how we show up today.

Once mistakenly regarded as having children from a previous relationship, being divorced, or not having a "good" childhood or history of "good" relationships, emotional baggage is the great leveler that, regardless of what we all think makes us so different or better or worse, we all have. None of us are exempt.

Thanks to being raised during the Age of Obedience plus society's previous lack of awareness of how our responses to our experiences, habits, and trauma can have a lifelong impact on our emotional, mental, physical, and spiritual well-being, we weren't taught how to manage our emotional baggage. As a result, most humans carry on as if they can accumulate and accumulate without dealing with it, often fearing what lies beneath. And this is understandable given that we've been systematically taught to distrust our feelings and plow on in the pursuit of acceptance and success.

But we have only so much space, and the same place we store joy, desires, and what we deem to be the good things in life is where we also store the past. There is no basement, attic, or spare room in our bodies to cram full of our dumped, disregarded, and buried experiences; it's all in the same "room." So when we think we're cleverly avoiding ourselves and dodging conflict, criticism, stress, rejection, disappointment, and loss, we're *adding* more baggage to the already unprocessed haul.

Our bodies aren't designed for hoarding unprocessed emotions and dodgy narratives that effectively cause us to lie to and neglect ourselves. We have only so much "space." There is no external hard drive to off-load what we don't want to deal with internally. If we think of our capacity as 100 percent and that everything's going in the same place, hauling around our hoarded grievances and guilt is like trying to operate at hundreds or even a few thousand percent. Nothing works effectively when overloaded, even we humans who carry on as if we're machines. And so we have to unpack, declutter, process, and tidy up by allowing ourselves to evolve with healthier boundaries that help us to heal, grow, and learn, otherwise our emotional baggage manifests itself in our health as well as our attitudes, thinking, behavior, and choices. When we get tipped over the edge into erupting and triggered over challenges (something we'll address with the final step, Learn from Eruptions and Challenges), it's a major clear out. That's why life-stage changes like parenthood, menopause, and career changes, along with breakdowns, burnout, breakups, redundancy, bereavements, and other losses, can be so triggering but also, if we let them, releasing.

If you want to know, like, and trust yourself; to enjoy healthier, mutually fulfilling relationships; to be open to welcoming more of the things and experiences that reflect who you really are, you are going to have to let go of some stuff. You can't take it all with you, much as you have tried, and your people pleasing is telling you that you are full.

You do not need to get rid of all of your emotional baggage. That's not possible, not least because we all continue to carry experiences and feelings. It's a sign that we are here. That said, you will not have to accumulate or store at the level that you are and have been if you cut back on people pleasing. You will have room to deal with life's challenges without feeling as if each thing that comes along causes you to teeter on the brink or tip over the edge and spiral.

Every time you ask, *What's the baggage behind this?* and you allow yourself to evolve your boundaries even a little bit, you are healing your emotional baggage and moving from the passive response of people pleasing to a more assertive, *active* response. This shifts your own energy and well-being and the dynamics of your interpersonal relationships, even if some of the people within them are living in the past.

Yes, therapy, exercise, yoga, journaling, meditating, treating yourself—you get the gist—are helpful, but if you don't learn to start saying no and allow yourself to create healthier boundaries, then you are cutting off the head of the weed without also taking out the root.

OUR RELATIONSHIPS HELP US TO HEAL, GROW, AND LEARN

Rather than confront our emotional baggage so that we don't become subsumed by it, we avoid it and build walls instead of boundaries. Our people pleasing is a wall we erected, our guardedness about exposing ourselves to the possibility of being hurt in the way we were before. It's a defense against the past that says, *I don't trust myself but I also don't trust you not to hurt me, so let me people-please you instead in the hope you won't.*

We think we're being boundaried when we tell people what to do or warn them about how other people have hurt us. What we're really saying though is, *I'm still hurt and angry, so if I warn you and please you, maybe you'll think twice about disappointing me.* We think we're loving people by trying to please them all the time or avoid conflict. What we're saying is, *I've been hurt, so I'm pleasing you by hurting myself so that you don't have any reason to reject or disappoint me.*

We keep trying to right the wrongs of the past by playing roles in the hope that we'll get our do-over, that people will finally figure out what they're supposed to be and do so that rather than it being us meeting their expectations and feeling shitty and shortchanged, they're complying with ours too. The idea is if we can make things happen in the way that we feel they should have, we will get the attention, affection, approval, love, and validation we've sought but not received. So we keep setting ourselves up for a fall with our far-out fantasy by hedging our bets on being happy via our people pleasing, all while piling up the baggage.

Our experiences are here to help us unpack, tidy up, and reclaim ourselves. See all these different experiences—the great, the good, and the not-so-great—that you've been through in adulthood? They all serve the purpose of trying to get you to confront your emotional baggage. Your interpersonal relationships in particular will push your buttons because of any habits of relating you learned in childhood, including the identities you took on with roles and how you do or don't create boundaries. They will cause emotional baggage to surface and reveal the old pain, fear, and guilt that you still harbor. This is not because you're "not good enough" but because you're being invited to see what you couldn't see before and stop using your maladaptive habit of people pleasing.

Your people pleasing shows you what's waiting to be resolved and healed so you can gain emotional peace. How you've seen yourself and how the world works represents old misunderstandings that you've responded to by becoming a people pleaser. Each time you've come up against life's inevitables, it's not because the world is trying to punish you or make you look stupid; it's trying to get you to say no. It's trying to get you to have boundaries so that you evolve your responses to reflect who you are in the present, the person you want to become, and the types of relationships and experiences you want to have. By shifting your responses and no longer being in the child role, you can't have the codependent attitude of people pleasing because you know your responsibility and recognize where you end and others begin.

You have outgrown your old identities. People pleasing no longer fits you. Healthier boundaries work better for you.

RECOGNIZE YOUR BAGGAGE BY PEOPLE-PLEASER STYLE

Gooders, who or what taught you that keeping up appearances and that being "good" would ensure that you got what you want or that nothing bad would happen to you?

Efforters, whom is it that you still crave attention, affection, approval, love, and validation from?

Avoiders, whom or what taught you to be the person who doesn't make things harder on anyone else?

Savers, whom didn't you get to save or help, or whom are you trying to be better at helping and saving than?

Sufferers, whom are you covering up for or whom is it that you're trying to get to notice, recognize, and acknowledge your pain?

Is this how you want to feel or be?

What can you see now that you couldn't see before?

HOW TO STAY IN YOUR LANE AND CLEAN UP YOUR SIDE OF THE STREET

All too often, the things that we dislike in others, that we want to change or have some level of control over, point right back at something we ourselves are doing or not doing. It annoys us, for example, that another person is being ambiguous, and so we decide to set a boundary with them about not being ambiguous without acknowledging our own ambiguity.

For boundaries to respect you and others, they need to be mutual. When you know (or think you know) what the boundary is for others, you need to reflect that in your own thoughts, behavior, and choices. This means that while you might have to say or show something to the person in question, you also need to address the boundary on your end even if they don't change their behavior in the way you would like.

If you don't acknowledge your part in the situation, no matter how small you perceive it to be, and don't shift anything on your side, you not only remain open to experiencing the issue(s) again in a similar way—that's life giving you the opportunity to address that pesky emotional baggage again!—but you also won't acknowledge the insight you stand to gain. Adjusting and evolving your boundaries so that they are not the same as the past will not only enrich your understanding of your-self and your experiences but also leave you feeling empowered to pro-ceed with an even slightly healthier boundary that you will continue to evolve over time.

Acknowledging your part is not about taking the blame and owner-ship of whatever it is that you dislike about the situation and the other person's contribution; it's about recognizing that you can truly know, con-trol, and amend only the scope of your own responses. That part, inciden-tally, might mean recognizing what you've said to or about yourself in response to the person's actions. Yes, they are a pain in the backside, they did you wrong, but if you're saying all sorts of shit about yourself and dragging around a painful narrative, that's on you. Trying to get other people to change so that you can feel better about how you're responding has a limited effect if you ultimately don't distinguish your baggage and boundaries from theirs.

You can choose how you want to conduct yourself and how you want to respond to feelings, thoughts, your own actions, those of others, and events, but what you cannot choose or control is what others think, feel, or do. You have to take care of your side of the street, and you have to be what you seek from others. This stops you from victimizing yourself by continuing to hold yourself hostage to a situation you dislike.

When you don't say no to what isn't working, you restrict your options to the following:

- Suffering in silence and/or people pleasing in an effort to keep the peace or to limit further encounters.
- Battling over who's right or wrong, trying to be the winner, or getting your payback.
- Cutting them off to avoid having boundaries, try to punish, or wrestle control.

When you clean up your side of the street irrespective of what the other person does, your options shift to these:

- Engaging from a more boundaried place and/or limiting the amount of time you spend with them (putting a bit of distance between them and yourself but not opting out).
- Engaging from a more boundaried place by opting out temporarily.
- Engaging from a more boundaried place by opting out permanently.

All these options are more boundaried and have a clear-cut agenda.

A mistake many make when attempting boundaries is seeing them solely as a means of guiding and directing or even ruling others, but boundaries are for you. Others know the line when you know the line. If a person isn't being boundaried, your behaving as though they *are* or that the situation is "normal" violates your boundaries and gaslights you. You need to evolve your boundaries to recognize the difference between someone with boundaries versus someone without them so that you take care of yourself but also so that the boundaries allow the natural consequences to take place.

Your boundaries are not contingent on whether others have boundaries. It's also, however, about no longer depleting yourself by doing for others what you're not willing to give yourself. You might consider yourself to be very compassionate, empathetic, tolerant, conscientious, and giving—people pleasers often are, to a fault—but if you withhold compassion, empathy, tolerance, thoughtfulness, and grace from yourself, then you're not really doing these for others; you're displacing. Compassion, empathy, and the like only work if they go in both directions, just like boundaries.

Gooders, where do you need to match your actions with your words and intentions instead of focusing on crafting an image?

Efforters, what are you trying to prove or get others to recognize, and which achievements, efforts, and accomplishments do *you* need to recognize and internalize?

Avoiders, where do you keep deferring to others and how can you use this to express a preference?

Savers, where can you take the energy you're putting into someone else and direct that at yourself?

Sufferers, how can you give yourself the same thing that you're trying to get from others?

EMBRACING HEALTHY BOUNDARIES

- Fear of having boundaries is a problem with having boundaries and *also* respecting other people's. You can't be afraid of boundaries while also claiming that you respect everyone else's. It's mutually exclusive.
- Getting a *no* is not a way of being punished, of having your suffering extended; it's simply *no*. Recognizing when you feel uncomfortable with *no* and boundaries connects you with the baggage behind your response so that you get to consciously choose a different, boundaried response.
- We can change our narratives. We don't have to accept the first draft that we made at the time of the original event. Recognizing the old misunderstandings in your emotional baggage isn't an opportunity to beat yourself up for being "wrong." You can't know what you know you don't know. Sometimes when we have negative associations with being wrong, we avoid updating the narrative because it will make us wrong. Sure, you've misunderstood some stuff, but accepting that you have allows you to make the right choices for your life that reflect a more honest version of events.
- Everybody has baggage, so in learning to recognize yours, you get to recognize where other people's baggage shows up in situations rather than personalizing their response.

If there's somebody you tend to get into the same arguments with or they trot out the same accusations and assumptions about you, instead of ruminating and internalizing it, catch yourself and say, *That's not my stuff; it's theirs, and I'm sending it right back.* Keep doing this and you will notice how you catch yourself before being drawn into unnecessary drama.

TROUBLESHOOTING *NO*

I feel really unsettled by my responses when something or someone triggers me, but it also feels too frightening and unsettling to try to connect with the baggage behind it. What can I do?

Work with a trauma-aware therapist who works with, for example, talk therapy, EMDR (eye movement desensitization and reprocessing), or forms of alternative therapy, so you have someone sitting alongside you as you gently address what's coming up for you but also so that you can calm your nervous system and put yourself in the position of being able to take additional steps to care for yourself. Remember, boundaries are your needs, expectations, desires, feelings, and opinions, so by allowing yourself to access support, you're saying no to continuing as is and yes to healing and breaking the cycle.

People who are aware of what I've been through aren't being sensitive enough to why I might find some of their boundaries difficult. What can I say to them?

Their having boundaries doesn't necessarily equate to being insensitive. You have to tread carefully with expecting people to adjust their boundaries to accommodate your discomfort with your own—for example, expecting people to automatically know and sense that you are passive so that they take the lead and don't ask too much of you. Your expectation might mean your needing them to have unhealthy boundaries by taking responsibility for you. Something we don't take into account when we expect others to keep making concessions is that everyone has emotional baggage and some of what we expect may be deeply triggering for them or reflective of an unhealthy role where they'll end up feeling guilty and try to appease us.

I feel like I'm always the one making the effort, including with boundaries. Aren't relationships supposed to be fifty-fifty?

Relationships are one hundred–one hundred, not fifty-fifty. We're humans who veer between exaggerating and underestimating ourselves, and there's no way of knowing what our "cut" is or what 50 percent looks like. We also cannot delete half of ourselves and expect the other person to fill in the blanks. So we have to do our best to be more of who we really are so that we then have a sense of whether we are in a mutually fulfilling relationship. When we focus on our cut, keeping score, and what we feel the other person is or isn't doing, we're going to people-please to over-compensate for where we feel they're not showing up but also to try to create a tipping point where we hope they might.

Okay, I can see that I have my baggage, but shouldn't people know that what they're doing is wrong?

We don't live in a world that's historically encouraged us to have healthy boundaries. Sometimes you haven't even registered that what someone is doing is wrong. Some people don't know because it's their habit and they've experienced limited consequences, and some do know and want to see what they can get away with. Even if the person does know, doesn't that mean that we also need to know? When we expect people to mind read or to use our good behavior to change their own behavior, we're having a passive instead of active response because we're avoiding vulnerability and responsibility.

How can I have boundaries with the people who have the same baggage as me but aren't dealing with their stuff?

Even if you're twins and spent all your time together, you still experienced things individually, and so you can't speak for all the other person's baggage or decide what they should or shouldn't be doing. Boundaries aren't about whether other people can handle them. Even when somebody does have similar baggage and responses, you have to be careful of projecting your feelings about yourself and your experiences onto them and be open to recognizing where they are coming from, aka empathy.

How do I start being more boundaried with family (or other long-standing relationships) when they expect me to be a certain way?

Everyone's boundaries are different, and we are each responsible for letting others know where we stand and where they stand with us—and, yes, that includes family. Due to the long-standing history, it's crucial to take responsibility for how you want to come across now and going forward because the concept of family relies heavily on habit and assumption. If you don't want them to think that past experiences of you or assumptions apply, you have to be more boundaried so that you have a clear differentiation between the past and the present. If you keep acting as you always have, even if inside you're about to erupt, your boundaries will be unclear. Also, even if you've said yes one thousand times to something that doesn't work, you're allowed to change your mind and start saying no. No one is entitled to a harmful *yes*.

I'm really close with this person. Aren't boundaries and saying no going to ruin that?

If you don't say no, if you're not truly honest about who you are and expressing your innermost feelings and thoughts, you're not as close as you think. No boundaries, no intimacy. This is a good time to check in with yourself about your associations with honesty. What's the baggage behind why you think increased authenticity will cause a problem? You are close and intimate only when you're willing to say and do things that run the possibility of conflict—and come out the other side.

10

REPARENT YOURSELF

That day back in August 2005 when I decided to explore other options following my shock prognosis, I walked out of the hospital without a plan. While on the Tube headed to work, I remembered a friend who'd mentioned how one of her forty cousins—big Irish family—had been through a terrible time with a mystery illness that baffled doctors. They had finally gotten answers and their health back after visiting a kinesiologist, a therapist who uses muscle testing and other techniques to identify the body's imbalances to help return it to health. Less than a week later, and I was sitting in an office embarking on a conversation that would change my life.

In my mind, the plan was that she'd identify my allergies and food intolerances (she did) and off I'd go. But Sonia asked about more than medical history and did more than muscle testing, checking the sources of stress in my body. I became uncomfortable. Not in a *she's violating my boundaries* way but more of a *I sense she's about to ask about things that I avoid* way. I felt the urge to bolt. "I, um, remembered that I need to get back for a, um, client meeting," I stumbled, unable to meet her eye with my barefaced lie. "It's okay," she said. And then I remembered I didn't want to die by the time I was forty, so I let her crack on.

The stresses she identified from specific periods in my childhood represented painful life events I'd shoved down. Among them, my mother giving birth to my little brother when I was twelve and coming home and cutting off my hair because she said it was breaking, claiming I hadn't cared for it properly in her few-days absence. Five-year-old me in a children's hospital for six weeks after a skin graft to remove a potentially cancerous birthmark, my father visiting only once, and my threatening to throw myself out the window after he left and having to be sedated.

"How do you feel about all of this?" she asked gently.

"Fine," I said in a singsong voice.

"Really?" she asked.

And then I broke down.

Minutes later, Sonia asked the question that changed my life, that galvanized me to want to change my life and subsequently learn to say no: "Do you think it's fair to blame a two-and-a-half-year-old for her parents' breakup or their subsequent behavior?" I didn't, but it hit me there and then that everything I did was essentially my blaming my younger self, Little Nat.

> Acknowledging the baggage behind your responses allows
> you to recognize your inner child and accept the experiences
> that caused you pain.

I don't know what's happened in your life, but I know stuff has. And even though maybe you've focused on more recent events or all the times you think your adult self "should" have known better, what you've been doing through people pleasing is expressing anger at your younger self while simultaneously trying to protect them from being hurt in the way that they were before.

We think we leave our younger selves behind in childhood, but they're still with us.

Imagine yourself as one of those *matryoshka*, Russian nesting dolls. Inside there's a version of you for every age, every moment you've been.

When you're disconnected from yourself because what you do on the outside is so at odds with who you are on the inside, reinforcing stress, those younger versions of you are unsettled and fearful. As your thinking, behavior, choices, and feelings reflect the past, those younger versions of you think that it is still the past. Remember, your subconscious doesn't tell the time, so if your adult boundaries don't either, as far as your body's concerned, you're still in threatening situations.

In an ideal world, our parents and caregivers would nurture, love, and support us into being fully realized adults by the time we become adults. They'd step back gracefully but also know when to step in. It would be smooth, and there would be no conflict, criticism, stress, disappointment, loss, or rejection. But we all know that's not how the world works. Your younger self is crying out for reassurance, for support, for their needs to be met, for emotional peace. What you need is what your younger self needed, and so you have to reparent yourself.

The biggest block to creating healthy boundaries and breaking the cycle is, whether consciously or not, continuing to think, feel, and act from a place of being in a child role in our interpersonal relationships.

> Reparenting is about connecting with the younger aspects
> of yourself that drive your pleaser so that you can finally
> give yourself what you need, fill the void, and stop trying
> to right the wrongs of the past. It's about regaining the ability
> to speak your feelings to yourself by entering into a more
> compassionate, honest, and present relationship with
> yourself.

Our people-pleasing patterns are about trying to meet unmet needs from the past and fill voids, but this prevents us from growing up because we're playing roles to fulfill the childhood fantasy of finally receiving the attention, affection, approval, love, and validation we seek.

Instead of hoping for a parent or caregiver (or somebody else significant who impacted your childhood) to change so that you can finally right the wrongs of the past, you can focus on taking on the primary responsibilities of parenting yourself.

While the idea of reparenting can seem like a daunting prospect, let's keep it real here: You've already parented yourself, just with dodgy boundaries, self-criticism, and withholding. You weren't consciously doing it as an extension of having healthier boundaries and allowing yourself to say no.

When you became an adult, you became your primary caregiver. That *doesn't* mean that your parents and caregivers cease to exist literally or figuratively and that you don't need anybody, but a transition of power needed to take place that allowed you to have agency to figure out who you really are so that you can be yourself.

If you accept that you are your own primary caregiver and empower yourself to say no, then it's no longer possible to be in a child role because you're acknowledging that you're an adult and how that needs to reflect your thoughts, actions, and choices and, in turn, change your feelings.

But because your inner child, your younger self, is within you, you need to take care of them, too, so that they stop taking over your life in unhealthy ways, trying to get you to fix the past. By nurturing these parts of you—your Russian dolls—your younger selves will start to calm, and you will feel safer and secure.

Parenting is about being or acting as a mother or father to someone, and you don't have to be their biological parent to do so. There are people in your life who were and are parenting figures but weren't necessarily your parents, and you can be that to yourself now and going forward. Just as your parents weren't born parents, you weren't either, which means that you have to learn on the go by taking up the challenge of updating your relationship with yourself.

You're not that kid anymore, so you no longer have to be powerless or helpless or stick to outdated and fake rules and obligations. This means you allow yourself to have the boundaries you didn't think you were allowed to have in the past, that you thought people would take issue with. Now that you're reparenting yourself, you don't have to follow suit and can choose a different way. Reparenting is self-care because it allows you to access the relationships, things, resources, activities, habits, and opportunities that let you healthily meet needs and become more of who you really are instead of depriving yourself or self-soothing in unhealthy ways.

BE AWARE OF WHEN YOUR INNER CHILD IS SHOWING UP

By asking, "What's the baggage behind it?" you have taken your first steps in recognizing, acknowledging, and taking care of your inner child. Whenever you play roles and avoid saying no, you are in a child role—that is, your inner child is present in some way. You'll know they are because you are . . .

- Feeling, thinking, and acting in ways similar to a much younger version of yourself.
- Compliant, on autopilot, obedient, and following rules even when it makes no sense or compromises or hurts you.
- Experiencing the people-pleaser feelings (anxiety, resentment, guilt, overwhelm) after avoiding *no.*
- Using reasoning habits—beliefs—that reflect childlike narratives and perspectives you haven't questioned or updated.
- Feeling inexplicably insecure, scared, anxious, and unsafe about getting into trouble, being ignored, doing the wrong thing, getting hurt, or being abandoned or rejected.
- Doing the same thing and expecting different results and trying to be the exception to other people's rules of behavior.
- Being passive-aggressive, masking feelings of frustration and resentment with outward compliance, or seeming okay while hinting at your true feelings with obstructionist and resistant behavior, even if subtle.

- Acting out because your ego's taken over, so you're trying to get attention; comparing; copying; trying to win, be right, or have the power; or are trying to get back at someone, even if indirectly.

Try to slow down and pause, and then ask, *What do I need? What am I feeling? How can I support myself?*

REPARENT YOURSELF
BY YOUR PEOPLE-PLEASER STYLE

Gooders might need to breathe out and not have to follow rules or focus on appearance so rigidly.

Efforters might need to breathe out and not have to try to keep up, perform, or prove.

Avoiders might need to breathe out and be allowed to ask a question and be curious.

Savers might need to breathe out and be allowed to ask for help and relinquish responsibility.

Sufferers might need to breathe out and know that someone (you) cares and is listening.

Our inner children, given that they represent our younger selves, also represent our more creative, playful selves. What can you do that allows you to tap into this? Each time you evolve your boundaries even a little and differentiate between the past and the present, it's an opportunity to take care of and do better by your younger self.

Recognize your role and your existing parenting style and adapt it to reflect a healthier boundary. You've begun to get a sense of the roles you play in your interpersonal relationships, including your people-pleasing style. How do these show up in the way you've parented yourself up until now? For instance, gooding might focus on parenting that emphasizes obedience, being good, and keeping up appearances; efforting will have a coach, pusher vibe to it; avoiding and suffering might be cautious, punitive, or shaming; and saving might involve guilting.

An easy way to recognize your parenting style is to consider how you were parented and where, in turn, you've effectively picked up the baton and adopted and continued that style as your own narrative. You now have an opportunity to consider the type of parent you want to be.

Even though you might dislike much of your parents' or caregivers' style, be careful of sliding to extremes. Sometimes, in our efforts to totally distance ourselves from parents and caregivers, we wind up feeling conflicted about having boundaries or beating ourselves up if we have so much as a whiff of similarity.

Here are some questions to help you explore your parenting style in your journal:

- What type of parent are you going to be?
- Which values will you teach?
- How will you set an example for your younger self?
- How will you deal with "tantrums" and acting out?
- How will you comfort and reassure your inner child?
- How will you help them learn, and how will you handle mistakes?
- How are you going to protect them without making either of you hypervigilant?
- How can you give your inner child freedom to explore and to express themselves?
- How can you give both of you a good standard of living, not "getting by" but also not purely focused on material goods?
- Where you've recognized that you haven't been taking care of yourself, what can you start to do? What's the next small step?

Distinguish between your inner critic and your inner voice. Each of us has an inner critic, the negative chatter we hear almost as a persona inside ourselves that we interpret as feedback that we are being or doing something wrong (or that we will be guilty of if we don't heed it). It is totally different from our inner voice, which is calm, respectful, and concerned only with the present.

Your inner critic will say whatever it takes to stop you from going out of your comfort zone. It reminds you of (and exaggerates) past mistakes, lest you risk doing it again, and it ultimately wants to control the uncontrollable because it's as if you need to know what will happen in 2099 so it (and you) can feel safe. Your inner critic thinks it's being helpful and keeping you on the straight and narrow, but think of this chatter as a backing track that's recorded vocals from previous experiences where you've internalized feedback, including criticism, rules, and obligations. This backing track plays behind the scenes like a radio on low or elevator music, and then the volume increases when you put so much as a pinky toe outside your comfort zone.

You've inadvertently mistaken your inner critic for your inner voice and let it be the boss of you, hence why you're so proficient at emotionally blackmailing yourself into avoiding healthy boundaries with your people pleasing. Like everything else you've hauled around, your inner critic is a habit. It automatically plays and becomes louder in contexts in which it's already used to playing—where you're afraid, critical, and judgmental. It's not that your inner critic is "right" or that it's even related to the events at hand—remember, your subconscious isn't based in the present, and the amygdala that handles fear can be a tad over-the-top at times—so it throws up what's already proved to be effective. That's why even though you're a grown-up, it's dragging up old shit about that time when you embarrassed yourself on the playground or using being scared of your parent to block you from speaking up at work.

Your inner voice is not repetitive, negative, emotionally blackmailing, nor does it sound like someone significant from the past, whether it's in tone or what it's parroting. It's neutral. It won't always tell you what you want to hear, but it will always have your back without it ever employing shame to give you a few kicks in the rear to make you compliant. But it *might* be a hell of a lot quieter than your inner critic because you don't typically listen to yourself, and people pleasing is like having your inner critic in the driver's seat.

It's also crucial to recognize where you use your inner critic as a substitute or coparent, and you need to claim your parenting rights. By having more of an active role and an active response, you will calm your inner critic. No, you won't be able to make them go away, as it's a protective device, but you will be able to sit alongside it and be like, *Oh, hello, old friend. Surprise, surprise that you've turned up to shit on me when I'm feeling good about myself.* (Can you tell I've said that to myself?)

Your inner critic is fear, and it is very overzealous. You always know that it's your inner critic, not your inner voice, because it's a contrary, switchy mofo. You do as it says, and it switches sides and has a go at you about that. It's never satisfied. If you stop trying to please it, you will become more authentic because you will allow yourself to grow up. You will also find that your inner critic relaxes and stops being so aggressive when you are more authentic because it is most active when you're out of integrity with your boundaries and values.

Talk to and regard yourself more kindly. It's time to give yourself more grace and recognize your humanness instead of reinforcing your inner child's fear that you are still in the past.

Is the way that you treat and regard yourself how you would want to parent yourself or a small child? Would you speak to or treat a loved one in the way you do yourself? If the answer to that is no, and I'd like to think it is if you've gotten this flippin' far in the book, you have no business treating and regarding yourself in the way you have—as if you don't matter. That little kid is still alive inside you. Depending on how you treat yourself, they might think they're still under siege with a bully or abuser or that no one cares or that someone who doesn't know "everything" is the boss of them.

Where are you impatient, intolerant, and lacking in compassion and empathy with yourself in ways you are not with others, and how can you level up?

Reparenting yourself involves sitting alongside yourself, and instead of judging or shutting down your inner child when they show up, you come from a place of curiosity and observation. You acknowledge why they're coming up—and then give them reassurance. When you feel rattled inside, that's what your younger self is looking for—reassurance that it's not the past, and affirmation from you that they are safe with you and that you care about their well-being. Because you've already begun to acknowledge where your baggage is showing up, rather than be impatient, intolerant, or disparaging of your younger self, you have started to gain some insight into what's going on.

When I talk to fellow people pleasers who are also parents and scared of repeating their own childhoods, time and again, I encourage them to have an ongoing dialogue. When a child has the freedom to talk to you about the small things, they'll build up to bigger things, especially when you allow them to feel safe or you're willing to course correct when you realize that you haven't had the ideal response. Having an ongoing dialogue, though, is also about noticing and getting dialed in to your child's habits so that you have a sense of where you need to be extra vigilant or meet a need. You can do this for yourself too.

Keep up an ongoing dialogue as you go about your life. Remember, just as your own parents and caregivers aren't infallible, neither are you, so you are allowed to make mistakes. You certainly don't have to make the same mistakes as your parents, but even if you do, you can learn from these because you have gained insights that show you a different route.

Healthily soothe yourself when you feel triggered by saying no. You have conscious and unconscious means of managing your thought, feeling, and action responses to the various situations you find yourself in. This is self-soothing, your ability to nurture yourself and respond to your needs.

Your collection of people-pleasing habits has been your way of relieving stress, anxiety, sadness, loneliness, anger, rejection, and insecurity, and trying to meet your various needs, but because it's a maladaptive strategy, it's become increasingly ineffective because it's not a healthy and helpful way of soothing. It provides temporary relief but ultimately creates more problems than it solves.

As you start saying no and being more boundaried, you will get a sense of when and why you need to comfort and support yourself. The aim of self-soothing is not about obliterating what you consider to be the source of the problem or shutting down your feelings. It's about feeling your feelings and then responding to them with something that healthily calms or neutralizes them so that you can then feel better within yourself or be in a space to figure out your next steps.

When you feel unsettled by saying no (or considering doing so), connect with the present and your body by saying, "I am safe, I am secure." Keep repeating. You're giving your body a chance to register your surroundings, including the year that you're in, so that it stops confusing what's happening with an old situation. I've also found that when I repeat this mantra, it means I'm not dwelling on the *no* or telling a story about the situation.

If saying no has stressed or upset you, whether it was doing it or the other person's response or what you fear might happen, this is where having a dialogue with yourself can be really soothing. Just as you would with a child, you let yourself get it all out, so vent the situation to yourself (or write it in your journal). Then, once you've heard yourself out, you gently shift yourself to another perspective that acknowledges your feelings and what you've said but allows you to see what's going on or what you might be able to do. You don't have to solve everything to the nth degree. We humans like to be seen and heard, and while we spend a lot of our bandwidth seeking it from others, we forget to give it to ourselves.

REPARENTING IS ABOUT giving yourself what you didn't get or giving yourself what you keep seeking from others, not because you don't need anybody else but because when you treat and regard yourself with love, care, trust, and respect, particularly at times when, in the past, you would have done otherwise, you will not accept less from others. You'll set the standard.

OBSERVE YOUR FEELINGS IN THE THIRD PERSON

When you're new to expressing and recognizing your feelings, it can seem quite daunting to say, for example, "I feel overwhelmed because I agreed to _____ and _____ because I was afraid of looking bad." You can practice stepping back by saying, for example, "[Your Name] is feeling overwhelmed because (s)he/they agreed to _____ and _____." This not only helps you observe, but because you're talking about your feelings in the third person, it can also help you calm down and get grounded (that is, self-soothe).[1]

BOUNDARIES ARE FORGIVENESS

A critical shift for me in my reparenting journey that also began in Sonia's office was acknowledging that parents aren't infallible. They do eff up, sometimes spectacularly so. They were once children themselves, and they are and were humans with interiors and backstories before we were even conceived. Inadequate parenting and caregiving in whatever guise that took doesn't equal an inadequate child.

Our parents and caregivers were raised in the Age of Obedience too. While they may have wanted better for us or were trying to do the best they could with the means they had, hence why they may have pushed too hard, focused on the wrong things, or had low and limited expectations of us, ultimately, they repeated what they'd learned without a fraction of the awareness and advice we're exposed to today.

Acknowledging our parents' and caregivers' humanness isn't an out. It's not about shifting the focus from our experiences to trying to find 101 ways to justify what did or didn't happen. Denying our experiences because of how we think it makes others look, not wanting to be disloyal, or trying to prove that we're grateful, or not wanting to face the truth, compounds our pain and adds more unprocessed emotional baggage.

To embrace the joy of saying no, of boundaries being a possibility for us, is to forgive ourselves. Boundaries are forgiveness because evolving our boundaries stops suppressing our needs, expectations, desires, feelings, and opinions, which forgives our younger selves. Forgiveness grants us permission to grow.

Humans have a complicated relationship with forgiveness, though, between what we may have learned through religion, the messages we received while growing up, and our habits of how we think we've been practicing forgiveness so far: "Say sorry"; "Don't bear grudges"; "Move on!" Forgiveness is often regarded as something we bestow on others, and we are seen as hard-nosed if we don't. People pleasing convinces us that we're very good forgivers. In reality, we're quick to let people return to business as usual while we privately beat ourselves up because we've absorbed the blame and shame of the whole thing.

Forgiveness is a decision to choose and keep choosing to let go by gaining perspective, and we gain perspective when we allow ourselves to be more truthful about what's going on, which is boundaries.

Forgiveness does not mean that you are condoning someone else's actions. It doesn't mean that you have to trust them again or engage to the same degree as before, especially if they've taken advantage of or even abused you. That doesn't mean that you haven't forgiven—it means that you've moved on and adjusted your boundaries accordingly. Forgiveness never means to press the reset button, nor does it oblige someone to change.

The childhood experiences that contributed to your people pleasing aren't your fault, but as an adult, the legacy of them and how they show up in your boundaries or lack of them is your responsibility.

Choosing boundaries chooses forgiveness. As boundaries are two-fold, by acknowledging what you need to do for yourself, you cannot be exposed to a situation in the same way as before because you have a different boundary and you're willing to learn in the future. You're also letting other people—as a result of what you're doing—own their behavior whether they choose to or not because you're not owning it by people pleasing, and so as a result they're not being sheltered from their behavior and how it impacted you and the relationship.

Along the way, every single one of us people pleasers lost ourselves and our *no*s. Some of us didn't get to be the children we feel we should have been or didn't get the nurturing, love, care, trust, and respect from our parents and caregivers. To let go of avoiding *no* is to accept that the past is done and to grieve for that kid that we didn't get to be, for the people our loved ones failed to be, but also for how hard we've been on ourselves.

Similar to the question Sonia asked me all those years go, do you think it's fair and reasonable to blame a small child for what you've criticized, judged, and even hated yourself for? Let the choice to have healthier boundaries, to say no, become an active way of trying to forgive yourself and the past as best as you can.

EMBRACE HEALTHY BOUNDARIES

- With reparenting, rather than reliving the past and inadvertently turning everything and everyone into versions of your parents and caregivers from whom to seek validation and a do-over, you enter into a more compassionate, curious, and nurturing dialogue with yourself and use healthier boundaries to parent those neglected parts of yourself.
- Boundaries reflect your values, with both acting as an internal guidance system that points to your needs, desires, expectations, feelings, and opinions. Having healthier boundaries than you did before and allowing them to evolve helps you make decisions and accurately assess and predict other people and situations. People pleasing disrupts, interrupts, and inhibits your internal guidance system.

- By embracing boundaries, you then have the maturity and emotional intelligence to handle relationships and situations outside of your previous comfort zone. You don't fear losing yourself because you own yourself.
- We cannot control the uncontrollable, but we can take command of ourselves.
- You might wonder why, for instance, a parent behaves one way with someone else but not you. Different person, different dynamic, different roles, different boundaries, *even if* you grew up in the same house and went through a lot of the same stuff. Your parent, when they behave this way toward you, often sees some of themselves in you and creates different expectations of you or fears the differences. Also, parents behave differently with people who aren't their children!
- Boundaries grow relationships by taking them to a more honest, nourishing place.

TROUBLESHOOTING *NO*

What are some quick and simple ways to connect with my younger self?

Look at old photos, or if you don't have any, try to picture what you were like back then. Do things you used to love doing as a child or that you didn't get a chance to do. Take your inner child on outings and show them around, or indulge in a treat you know would delight them. Include your inner child in what you're doing. *Eight-year-old me would have loved this!* Acknowledge when you lose yourself in the pure joy of doing something. When I dance, I'm my teenage self raving at the discos in Dublin and feel at one with the music. It's pure joy.

I feel like I've been taking care of myself my whole life, and I'm tired. I don't think I can do this.

I hear you. When you've been neglected, abandoned, or mistreated, or had to parent the adults or children around you even though you were a child yourself, you feel old before your time. You're so tired, you want to hand off to someone else and feel taken care of for once, and maybe you want to give people who inadequately parented and cared for you a chance to step up. If you start caring for yourself, it means they might not feel the need, the impetus, the guilt. You fear you're letting them off the hook. There might also be a part of you that doesn't believe you deserve to meet your own needs and wants, have standards, and give value to your feelings and thoughts.

You are your primary caregiver, though, and have been since you became an adult, and that's the case regardless of your experiences growing up. This doesn't mean that you do everything on your own; it means that you don't make your existence about payback or punishment. How about letting yourself off the hook? Withholding the self-care of *no* and boundaries is akin to giving yourself a life prison sentence. You don't deserve that. Reparenting yourself means you allow yourself to access the resources, support, and boundaries that will give you enough energy to start caring for yourself and evolving your relationships and choices to ones that support you instead of hurting you.

I've already made mistakes with my children, so how on earth can I reparent myself when I've failed them?

First off, who hasn't made mistakes with their children? If you hadn't, I'd be worried. I know there's a shit ton of parenting books out there, but there is no manual that will substitute for learning on the go. You parented from the level of awareness you had at that time, and, yes, like all parents do at some point, you find yourself being the parent you insisted you'd never be. Rather than hide from these missteps that are part of the parenting experience or beat yourself over the head with them, confront them and what these tell you about the baggage you need to face. Ask yourself, *What is this experience giving me an opportunity to confront?* By allowing yourself to see what you couldn't before about yourself and past experiences, you get to heal, grow, and learn.

Reparenting yourself will allow you to shift the dynamic of the relationship with your child(ren).

When I found myself acutely triggered when one of my children struggled with anxiety and panic attacks during the pandemic, shame and fear pushed me into hypervigilance that left me walking on eggshells, which only exacerbated the situation. Acknowledging what was coming up for me (the baggage behind it) and also what her anxiety mirrored made me realize that I had been afraid of myself because I saw a younger version of myself in her behavior that I had entirely forgotten about. And as soon as I did this, not only could I start taking care of this aspect of myself but I could be there for her too, and both of our anxieties eased.

When I try to have healthier boundaries, it feels like I'm hurting and rejecting the person. If they're not capable of the boundaries I need, aren't I loving the person conditionally or opening myself up to more drama?

Avoiding boundaries is not love. That's the childlike thinking where we imagine parents never saying no as the ideal or their spontaneously combusting into who we want them to be so we can live happily ever after. Boundaries communicate that you're treating yourself and others with love, care, trust, and respect and are aware of limits. Ironically, we have *more* freedom with boundaries, not *less*, because we (and others) have the freedom and flexibility to be ourselves. Without boundaries, you're denying reality and refusing to accept who they are. Unconditional love is loving someone through all seasons and conditions, not loving someone no matter what they do to you. Be careful of infantilizing and enabling. It's not for you to decide what boundaries they're capable of; decide and live yours. Unless you consistently have boundaries, you won't know the true nature of your relationship.

Being more boundaried is not about trying to change or rule others; you can be more boundaried regardless of whether someone else is or not. You can have a healthy relationship with someone by having a healthy attitude about them. It's recognizing and honoring the fact that you're two individual entities, that they're not the boss of you, and that they have only as much power as you afford them. It doesn't mean that you're both relating to each other healthily, but from your end of things, you respect yourself and them with healthy boundaries even if they don't have the common sense, empathy, or even character to do the same back.

I've tried having boundaries with this person, but they become so punitive, angry, and abusive. I feel like I'm going to have to walk away, but it feels so hard.

Some people, because of their own baggage, not the validity of your boundaries, are not in a position to have a remotely healthy relationship with anyone, never mind themselves. I know it feels as though holding on, not having boundaries, or trying to get them to stop mistreating and hurting you so that you can feel better, or similar efforts can seem like the way to go and that maybe you don't want to hurt, anger, or abandon them. Without boundaries, though, including ones that mean keeping a healthy distance or staying away, the person doesn't experience the natural consequences of their behavior. You keep taking responsibility for their responsibilities, they keep putting theirs on you, and you don't take responsibility for yourself. Of course it feels hard. You've been through a lot with this person, but don't confuse trying to get a return on investment and trying to make them change with a reason to stay or with loving and caring for them.

Recognize the baggage that's coming up for you and what the similarities are between this person and someone else significant from your past. When we want to change but feel disloyal or as if we're doing something wrong, it's because it represents a pattern we learned in our childhood dynamics.

Let's say that you do have to let go of a relationship because of their resistance to healthy boundaries. What other relationships might that make room for? What are you opening the door to? It's only by letting go of our ideas of what we think relationships *should* be—the pictures we've painted in our minds—and accepting who they are and have been that we can discern whether we also need to let go of the relationship altogether and stop interacting with that person.

I've always considered myself to be X type of person and feel that boundaries inhibit this.

Healthy boundaries express who you are. I often hear from people who say, "Natalie, I'm a high-strung or very spontaneous person, so I feel like I'm being fake." You're human, and so you're attached to certain characteristics and qualities as part of your identity, but what if you're more than what you're trying to define yourself by? If you really believe you're something, you will be able to do that *with* boundaries that allow you *and* your relationships to grow rather than keeping yourself small and stuck in habits that aren't serving you.

11

MAKE IT A DESIRE, OR SAY NO

At my father's funeral, as we listened to family members sharing stories of how he'd drop everything (including his wife and children) to come to their aid no matter the time of day, it hit me and my brother that we'd never stood a chance. It's no wonder Dad wasn't the father we'd needed or wanted—he didn't have the bandwidth and was stuck in his own cycle of people pleasing. Knowing the toll it had taken, including alcoholism and estranged and strained relationships, that day I vowed to stop doing things from a place of guilt.

As we gain awareness of how we spend our bandwidth, understand where and why our baggage is showing up, and begin reparenting ourselves by gradually shifting our attitudes to more compassionate ones that take us into consideration, we can find ourselves wrestling with knowing when to say no and deciphering what it is that we need or want to do.

Of course, given that we've been in our people-pleasing habits for most or all of our lives to some degree and so have oriented ourselves toward prioritizing other people's needs, desires, expectations, feelings, and opinions, this can feel foreign and unsettling. We feel unsure of what qualifies us to say no and of what our feelings tell us about what we do or don't want to do because we've learned to distrust and not listen to our feelings. And what about our obligations and what others expect of us?

And so we can find ourselves straddling two opposing problems where we don't want to keep doing things for the wrong reasons or that leave us feeling shitty about ourselves and our relationships, but we also don't want to tank our relationships and find ourselves all alone.

Let's say it from the top: If we don't say yes authentically, we say it resentfully, fearfully, or avoidantly, and this leads to far more problems than if we'd said no in the first place. This means that we need to *make it a desire, or say no*. The gap between what we want to do and obligations or other people's expectations is where tension, friction, and resentment reside.

> Notice how you feel and what you're thinking when you're about to do something, whether it's asked of you or something you expect of yourself or have decided to do. *Does it feel like a desire, or does it feel like an obligation or rule?*

The big clue is how you are feeling and thinking, including *should*s and whether your concerns center on how you will look to others. That's not about what you want to do.

THINK ABOUT SOMETHING you wanted to do. How did that feel in your body? Even if you were a little nervous, what were you thinking? This is an example of when you want to do something, so you have a pretty good idea of what wanting to do something feels like. This is not what obligation, rules, or emotionally blackmailing yourself into something feels like. It's not how you feel when you comply instead of consent.

Keep in mind that the more of your time, energy, effort, and emotions spent saying yes inauthentically, the less bandwidth you have. Being more discerning with your *yes* protects your well-being because you understand the link between *yes* and *no* rather than seeing them as distinct from each other.

OBLIGATIONS, *TECHNICALLY*, ARE about what we feel morally and legally bound to do, our senses of our duties and commitments, but thanks to the Age of Obedience, our senses of obligation extend far beyond this and so we tend to *feel*, *think*, and *behave* obliged around anyone we perceive to be an authority and where our people pleasers are activated.

As people pleasing is our emotionally blackmailing ourselves into doing stuff, we tend to feel obliged when we become aware of other people's needs, expectations, desires, feelings, and opinions, and so we feel duty-bound, but much of what we consider to be obligations are fake ones. They're often rules, *should*s we've taken to abiding by as foregone conclusions no matter how arbitrary, inappropriate, or irrelevant they might be. These create our senses of moral obligation because we think they're our characters and fear letting ourselves (or others) down and getting into trouble.

We use rules (our own and other people's) to make us feel safe and to protect us against the past happening again, but all they do is create more guilt and fear because in following the rules in this way, we live in fear of being "wrong" or hurt, and so we remain stuck in the past. We also wind up with a disproportionate sense of wrongdoing, leading to our believing we've done more bad things than we have or that we're hurting people with our *no*s.

Here's the deal: Each and every time you do something from a place of guilt, fear, or obligation, it *always* leads to resentment. Maybe not today, maybe not tomorrow, but soon.

Resentment is our anger, the emotional result of believing we were forced or expected to be or do something that we didn't want. Even if the person didn't force, emotionally blackmail, or oblige you, doing things because it's what you think is expected of you, not because you want to based on who you are, creates resentment because, invariably, you wind up feeling shortchanged.

> You have to make it a desire or say no because obligation is
> too closely associated with being a child and people having
> authority over you and the power to make you safe or unsafe.
> If you don't consciously choose what you do and don't want to
> do, your nervous system will not know the difference
> between the past and present.

When you do things from a place of obligation instead of consciously consenting to do so, you act as if you have no agency, no say in your circumstances, as if you're still that little kid. And so you violate your boundaries and your bandwidth doing things that exploit you or cause you to be out of alignment with your values, your character, and how you want to live your life.

Sometimes, you fear saying no because you know with every fiber of your being that this is exactly how you feel and it feels almost selfish to honor those feelings and disappoint someone else. When you're overattuned to other people's feelings, when they voice a request to you, you interpret it as an obligation for you to meet.

As we learned in chapter 2, compliance is being excessively prone to agreeing to obey others, and this means you comply even when you don't need or want to, and when you shouldn't. That's much of what creates your pain and problems right there because when you people-please more than occasionally, you don't merely do it with people who would do you harm or have a problem with your boundaries; you do it regardless because you're already in your role and often gravitating to people and situations that fit it.

There is a world of difference between compliance and consent. When you consent, you consciously and autonomously agree. You know what you are agreeing to and why. While compliance does mean that you "consent" by omission of the direct agreement or through silence or inaction, it's not consent; it's obedience. You've gone along with something as if you don't have agency, or you've gone along with something on autopilot and only later registered the impact.

When you react instead of respond, on some level you feel and behave as if you're responsible for other people's moods, feelings, and problems, which is codependency. You feel excessively emotionally reliant on this person for definition and safety and struggle to discern your responsibilities because you've merged your needs, desires, expectations, feelings, and opinions with theirs by suppressing and repressing yours to take care of their feelings and behavior.

People cannot know a line and a limit you don't create, even if you think that they "should." By making it a desire—by consciously choosing to do it even when it's maybe not your absolutely most favorite thing—you upgrade yourself to being a grown-up and acknowledge where you end and others begin.

CAN YOU GIVE ENTHUSIASTIC CONSENT?

Marie Forleo, entrepreneur and author of *Everything Is Figureoutable,* is known for saying, "If it's not a hell yes, then it's a hell no!" While this saying can be true in some instances, sometimes our *yes*es will be for things that we're moderately into. Not everything can be *oh hell yeah*. Sometimes it's a moderate *yes*, possibly because we don't know what's involved, we haven't got a lot of bandwidth left, or it's a so-so thing that we're okay to consent to. The key is to also start noticing what *no* feels like and using that data to help you trust your intuition and your boundaries so you can have your own back.

When you're aware of someone else's need, want, or expectation or are considering being or doing something, check in with yourself by asking these questions:

What am I feeling?

What am I anxious about?

What am I thinking?

Am I trying to control how I'm perceived?

Notice your feelings and acknowledge where even if you might *want* to do something, your people-pleaser feelings have emerged. Due to your pleaser habit, you've sometimes guilted yourself when, in actuality, you would do it *without* being shamed or threatened. As a result, you might be so used to doing things from a place of guilt that it's muddied the waters. It's not that you don't want to do things for your loved ones, but you may have such a disproportionate sense of what you're obliged to do that other people's expectations can be exhausting and stressful even when you might want to do something.

IF YOU'RE SELF-CRITICAL and trying to convince, push, shame, or berate yourself into doing something; if your thoughts are about what someone might say about you if you don't do it, catastrophizing, fuming about people asking or expecting you to do something, wanting to control, win, be right or not lose, halt. These are all messages from yourself that on this basis, you need to say no. If you were to go ahead right now, it would be for the wrong reasons.

I come across so many people who agree to help out, do extra and/or unpaid work, and take part in things they don't want to do. *All of them* had thoughts about how people might perceive them if they said no, emotionally blackmailing themselves into doing these things for the wrong reasons. What they don't consider is the impact, the meaning and consequences of agreeing to things in this way, including how negatively they perceive themselves and how they're effectively robbing their own bandwidth.

What you're thinking, feeling, and doing all more than qualify you to say no because, otherwise, you'd be doing whatever it is for the wrong reasons even if it's a supposedly "good thing."

Make it a desire, or say no.

> Train yourself to notice the things you're not into. I say, "Hard pass," in my head and have a giggle to myself.

MAKE IT A DESIRE BY YOUR PEOPLE-PLEASER STYLE

Gooders, notice where you think saying yes will make people feel good or think well of you in that moment, and look past that to what it is you genuinely want.

Efforters, notice where you would do something even if no one was around to acknowledge it and where you light up while doing something or even at the thought of it.

Avoiders, notice where you're tempted to defer to the other person and use it as a cue to pause and tune into your personal preference.

Savers, notice where something is genuinely mutually beneficial as opposed to your being in the role of giver.

Sufferers, notice the things you don't have to suffer through doing or agreeing to—and follow that feeling more.

GETTING A HANDLE ON OBLIGATION AND RESENTMENT

What do I *want* to do, and what do I feel *obliged* to do?

The obligation may be real in that someone else expects it of you and has communicated that it's a duty, but it can be that you feel obliged even though you are not because you've made it a *should*.

If there's a difference between your desire and obligation, *this* is the breeding ground for resentment. You must do the following:

- Close the gap by moving closer to what's authentic (the want).
- Convert the obligation to a desire.
- Communicate that you believe that this is an obligation.
- Or you need to say no.

For instance—and this is a common scenario that my clients deal with—let's say that your parents expect you to call every day. When you consider what you want to do versus the obligation (speaking every day), and you acknowledge that maybe you want to speak to your parents two or three times a week or not feel as if it has to be set in stone and that you can call whenever you like, being expected to make daily calls is a problem. You're doing double what you're comfortable with. Your desire for less isn't due to being a Bad/Mean/Ungrateful Child; you're having these calls for the wrong reasons and overriding your boundaries.

Find a healthy motivation to continue daily calls that has nothing to do with keeping up an identity or an ulterior motive so you remove or calm down the guilt and obligation and turn it into a desire, or say no to the obligation and dial things down. For example, at least start working your way to a middle ground or setting boundaries with yourself about how much time you spend on these calls.

Here's something that people pleasers often forget in their quest to please: Most people don't like feeling that you did something out of guilt or obligation *even if*—and I know it can seem absurd—they did guilt or oblige you into doing it. And I say "most" because some people don't care how miserable you are. They want you to comply and enjoy leveraging your conscientiousness and fear, and you need to have really good boundaries around these kinds of people. But if that's not who they are and they respect boundaries (or would if you gave them half a chance to know yours), then it's an insult to your relationship with them. Doing things from a place of obligation will put you in a child role and keep the relationship at a lower level of maturity. You will act out with passive-aggressive behavior, such as turning up late, being moody, or doing something badly.

It doesn't mean they'll be thrilled about it when you say no or can't or don't want to do something, but that's okay. You aren't thrilled when people say no to you! But these people would hate to think that the only or primary reason you engage with them or do as they ask is because you feel as if you *have* to.

Use doing things from a place of desire to treat yourself *and* others with dignity. Give them a bit of grace by not assuming the absolute worst of them (unless they are that) and extend some trust with your boundaries that they'll be able to handle their own feelings about it.

TEST YOUR MOTIVES

If I were to go ahead and do this and I didn't get the hoped-for or expected response and reward, would I still want to go ahead and do this? If the answer is no, you need to revise your motivations to something that reflects desire, a conscious choice, without an expectation of what you will get back, or you need to communicate your expectations to this person so that you can each proceed from an emotionally responsible place. If you can't do either, you need to say no.

Am I trying to get or avoid something? If the answer is yes, try to get as honest as possible with yourself about whether your approach is a boundaried way of going about it or a way that represents your people-pleasing habit that avoids being too vulnerable.

Here are four steps to help you have an assertive response when you recognize that you need to say no.

1. **Work out what you want to do versus what you think the other person expects of you or any generalized obligation.** Pay attention to those messages from your body, thoughts, and even actions that suggest that you don't want to do something or that a further conversation or form of action is needed. Give yourself the space and grace to get a sense of what you're feeling.
2. **Work out what you want to do and what that requires you to communicate.** This shifts you from having a passive response (in which you're aware of your discomfort or true thoughts and needs, but either not doing anything or dropping hints about it) to an active response.
3. **Identify your desired assertiveness outcome.** What do you need to achieve assertively? For instance, I say, "I don't want to do that." I communicate to my friend that "I'm going to [insert plan]." It could be that you voice an idea in the weekly meeting or talk about what's bothering you or ask for help.

Desired assertiveness outcomes cannot be about trying to control other people's feelings and behavior! If your objective is to make someone say X, think Y, or do Z, you're giving up your power and your boundaries—and you're also people pleasing.

4. **Communicate what you want or your position.** But go easy on the fluff. There's no need to pad out what you need to say with a load of excuses or story. People miss the point! They simply want to know where they stand (and where you do). Start lean and then add in detail. (For help, see the section about hard and soft *no*s in chapter 12). If you're not sure what you want, then it's okay to say that. Don't railroad or emotionally blackmail yourself into agreeing to something or let someone else do that to you.

THE POWER OF THE PAUSE

We can't control all of life's inevitables, but we can choose how we respond. Every day, every choice is an opportunity to make a new choice. Taking even a teeny bit of time to pause interrupts long-held habits of thinking and behavior. A pause allows you to take in your surroundings, to recognize where you are, to remember that your boss is not your parent, your partner isn't the enemy, or that you're not that kid anymore. You also need to insert a pause if you're inclined to say yes by default. Set an agreement with yourself that no matter who it is, whenever someone makes a request, or you're compelling yourself to say yes to something, that you will pause for at least ten seconds and recognize how you're feeling. If it doesn't feel good to say yes, it's time to park the *yes* or say no right there and then.

Let me get back to you is a magic phrase that gives you the space and grace to consider yourself. If you tend to say yes reflexively or when you really mean *no*, make it a personal rule for the foreseeable future that you use this phrase so that you have time to check in with your bandwidth and get a sense of what you want to do. Give yourself time to notice the thoughts and concerns that come up as well as feelings that you typically paper over quickly with a *yes*. In doing so, you will become more conscious, aware, and present. If the person says that they need an answer right now, then it's a *no*. Boop, there it is. Some people want to catch you unawares. And some people think they can't handle waiting and delaying their gratification. You won't know this if you don't give yourself time.

NOTE TO THE KINDHEARTED GIVER

A big fear with us people pleasers is that saying no will turn us into cold-hearted, selfish, unempathetic assclowns and that no one will want to be around us anymore. People pleasing is so intertwined with our identities that we fear being nothing without it even if we're pretty miserable with it.

Saying no isn't going to kill your spirit and stop you from being all the things you pride yourself in being. You can still be all the good qualities you value *with* boundaries, otherwise you are not being as much of these things as you think.

Here's the deal (and brace yourself): If you don't feel good after you give or help, then it isn't giving and helping. If you haven't got two beans of self-esteem to rub together even though you're the Most Empathetic, Compassionate, Conscientious, and Kindhearted Person Ever, then you, again, have not been giving.

Giving is the full transfer of something.

If you have an expectation of what the person should be, do, think, or feel in return, *it's not giving*. You have a hidden agenda and are sacrificing yourself to influence and control the other person's feelings and behavior in the hope of being rewarded with what you need. That's a contract, and when you have an expectation of what should happen *in exchange* for your contribution, the other party needs to know about this so that each of you can make emotionally responsible decisions about how to proceed.

Now, a part of you might be like, "Natalie, that's a bit harsh. Doesn't everyone expect something back when they do something?" Yes, but also no.

As humans, we like to receive recognition, acknowledgment, and appreciation for our efforts. They're part of our emotional needs. But if we do things in the pursuit of these and also have an expectation of what we're going to get back, we overstep boundaries.

As uncomfortable as it is for you and every people pleaser, including myself, to hear, an agenda is manipulation. And humans, including you, do not like feeling that they're being manipulated whether it's through abusive, forceful behavior or people pleasing's passive and passive-aggressive behavior.

> By making it a desire instead of an obligation or even a sacrifice, we stay in our lanes.

But what about making sacrifices for loved ones? Even when something is a sacrifice because we park something of ours to meet another's greater priority, when we do it from a conscious, boundaried place, it's no longer a sacrifice; we're giving autonomously. We have awareness of who we are and what we're being, doing, and giving, and so we know our boundaries and bandwidth. We're not keeping score. Sacrificing *yourself* is not giving; it's self-harm. There's no need to make ourselves bankrupt in any sense of the word in order to help out. That is too big an ask, and it's definitely not an obligation. It also can't always be you making the sacrifices and giving. If you're always the giver, everyone else is a taker.

EMBRACE HEALTHY BOUNDARIES

- Every time you play a role, you are either fitting around someone else's role or you're trying to get the person to change. You then feel resentful because complying instead of consenting leaves you feeling shortchanged, or the other person doesn't fulfill their side of the obligation and become who you want them to be.

- Lose the focus on what you will get back in return, and you will be surprised by how many "obligations" and "rules" drop off your roster and out of your bandwidth. When you have no attachment to what you're going to get back, you operate based on who you are.

- As a general rule of thumb that covers the overwhelming majority of situations, if you don't have an active response and assert your boundaries in situations where you need to represent yourself, your silence/compliance/inaction will be taken as a *yes*. Be very careful of what you cosign.

- Although sometimes you're saying, "No, not ever," most of your *no*s are more like, "Not right now." There's no need to behave as if saying no means you're saying full stop no to that person forever. It's simply *no*.

- You don't have to change what you want just because someone else wants something different.

- Just because you sense or know that someone has a need, it doesn't mean you're obliged to fulfill it. It's not *your* need.

- If you want some of your future *no*s to become easier, say no now and going forward. Your *no*s don't need to be perfect. Your *no* could be legit as can be and you could say it nicely, and someone could still take issue with it. Go ahead anyway.

TROUBLESHOOTING *NO*

How do I get a loved one to stop guilting me into doing stuff?

Whether a loved one coerces us into doing something, acts as if we've hurt them by not doing X, or treats us as if we're responsible for their feelings, being guilted feels unpleasant and is a guaranteed breeding ground for resentment. Here's a handy script that communicates what is happening, how it's felt and perceived, what needs to stop or happen, and what you value. Tweak it to suit your needs.

"When you say [insert no more than three specific and as close to verbatim examples as possible] or do [insert no more than three brief and specific examples], it feels like you're guilting me, and I don't like feeling this way. If you want me to do something, ask. You don't need to activate my conscience. If I can or want to do it, then I'll say so, and if I can't or don't want to, I'll let you know. I know it might be hard to hear, but I don't want to wind up feeling resentful. I value our relationship and want to feel as if [e.g., I can enjoy spending time with you], and that's why I'm telling you this."

Don't we have to "grin and bear it" sometimes? Surely we can't say no to everything we don't want to do?

In all areas of our lives, sometimes we've got to do things that we're not crazy into. That's called life, and sometimes we're not thrilled about doing certain tasks, but they facilitate other aspects of our lives and help us healthily meet our needs. We feel happy to do them because we're giving to ourselves and our priorities. We have the energy and the boundaries to do so. Inadvertently martyring ourselves with people pleasing, on the other hand, means we're always "grinning and bearing it." When we cut back on people pleasing, we have more bandwidth to do things that aren't only at the top of the list because we're not doing things that should be at the bottom or not even on there.

Does this mean that I don't have to do anything for my family? Because that feels harsh.

No. We are obliged to help our families out on occasion, but we can do so with boundaries by recognizing the obligation and meeting it from a place of desire. For example, my brother experienced a mental health crisis and turned up at our home unexpectedly, which is nearly two hundred miles from his. Even though it was the day before the girls went back to school, the following morning, I got up at 6:00 a.m. and drove him home. Was it convenient? No. Was I tired? Sure. But I did it because I could, and I wanted to. I made sure I buffered myself with extra self-care to restore my bandwidth and adjusted my commitments in the subsequent days so that I didn't behave as if I hadn't been through that big event.

Sometimes I don't feel like doing something but I make myself go. Sometimes I enjoy myself; sometimes I don't. How do I know when I want to?

While there's undoubtedly value in pushing ourselves on occasion to go out when all we want to do is do nothing, there's little value in doing so when we end up resenting the people we're around and disliking ourselves even further. We need to know the line between encouraging ourselves out of our comfort zones and not listening to ourselves. This is why taking the time to understand your bandwidth and your intentions matters. Try to discern the difference between the times you enjoy and the ones you don't. Gather the data. I met my now husband at an event I didn't really want to go to because it didn't sound appealing—it turned out to be great—because my friend begged me to join her. I didn't go grudgingly. I realized I wanted to. But other times, even when people have really wanted me to join them, if I know I'm super pooped, grumbling in my head, and starting to feel anxious and tight in my body, it's a hard pass. Ultimately, it's trial and error. Sometimes you will miss out on things, sometimes you will wish you gave something a miss, and sometimes you'll be so glad that you were pleasantly surprised.

I know I need to say no, but I feel so guilty and so I end up saying yes or backtracking after I've said no. Why do I feel so guilty?

Real talk: You feel guilty because it's a feckin' surprise that for a moment, you considered yourself. It's not that your boundaries are wrong or that you're doing something wrong; you are in unfamiliar territory. Your body is telling you that it has very little data on you healthily and authentically meeting your needs. The guilt feelings don't reflect the actual situation; it's a habit. It's the feeling your body is trained to throw out when you're in these contexts. So acknowledge the feeling, remind yourself of the truth of what's going on here, and keep going ahead and saying no where you can and self-soothing like we talked about in the reparenting chapter, and soon you will realize that you're okay.

I feel guilty about being off work or not being able to do something due to illness, maternity leave, burnout, bereavement, and so on. How do I know if it's time to go back?

If the same voice that talked you into doing things that were not in your best interest in the past is the same one making you guilty, it's *not* time. Or, you need to try to tap into what you want to do. It's okay to have time off. You are not a burden or lazy. Generally speaking, people pleasers need to take more time than they're comfortable with so that they go past the point of giving in to their inner critic and are more aligned with their needs and bandwidth.

How do I know if someone's request or expectation is unfair and unreasonable?

If doing, being, agreeing to, or putting up with something isn't going to cause you more problems by negatively impacting you, knock yourself out.

The right, healthy, compassionate thing to do for a situation is not always going to be what the other person wants or even you want. Say no to unfair and unreasonable because sometimes what you expect out of yourself *isn't* respectful of you either. Sometimes all someone needs out of situation is a clear *no*—then you'll both know where you stand.

12

CUT BACK
ON HINTING

In the eighteen months between getting engaged and married, I had a series of awkward conversations and meetings with my father where I dropped hints with wedding chat to nudge him to make his position known. When, after a year of reality-show-style big pauses and feeling my heart break a little more each time, he still didn't say anything, I opted to take this as *his* hinting that he knew it would be my stepfather who'd raised me since I was six years old walking me down the aisle and that he didn't give enough of a shit to step up and have the awkward but necessary conversation to clear the air. One month before the wedding, my aunt asked about my father's wedding suit, and the awkward albeit obvious truth about my stepfather's role came out, immediately starting a bonfire of conflict and forcing all the subjects the entire family had avoided out into the open.

If you want somebody to do what you want, give you what you need, or meet certain expectations, there are various options for going about it, including doing favors and making concessions so that they potentially might feel obliged to reciprocate in the way you want, need, or expect. Other ways include being manipulative, being obstructive, being kind, doing good deeds, letting them use you, and looking pained, to name but a few. As a result, when you do anything like these, it limits your options to hinting or being shady.

Do you know what we're doing with people pleasing? We're showing other people how to behave by using "being good" to communicate what we need, want, expect, feel, and think without coming out straight and being direct and assertive, but we're also trying to model how others "should" behave so that they will change their feelings and behavior. It's hinting, which, when it isn't providing clues for a game or a (fun) surprise, is a form of passive and passive-aggressive communication where we attempt to say something without saying it to avoid vulnerability and anything that might lead to rejection. This attitude of people pleasing creates a debt we expect others to pay off, and this includes our unspoken words that we expect others to mind read.

Here's the truth: On some level, I'd hoped that my father would take almost thirty-five years of my excusing his absence and lack of effort and spare me from spelling out that I'd including my stepfather in the wedding. I wanted him to tell me that he knew how painful and difficult both his absence and the decision were for me and how he'd love to be involved in any capacity he could. And do you know what? It's not the wildest expectation, but it was an unrealistic one of my father based on who he was. That, and I was avoiding my own responsibility and out of step with my integrity.

BECOME MORE AWARE OF YOUR PEOPLE-PLEASER HINTING

Gooders drop hints by continuing to be "well-behaved" to set a good example even when they're fuming inside at assholic behavior.

Efforters drop hints by trying to say and do the "right" thing with effort or by showing the strain of all their efforts.

Avoiders drop hints with "subtle" passive aggression, all while saying nothing's wrong.

Savers drop hints by sacrificing through helping and supporting and then by showing the strain of their sacrifice.

Sufferers drop hints by suffering to call attention to their need and then by suffering to highlight how they're being mistreated.

WHY DO HUMANS HINT? Because we think it's less scary to go some of instead of all the way. We don't want to hurt feelings, and we're hoping that people will figure out what we think, feel, need, desire, and expect without our having to put ourselves out there. That's why instead of coming out straight and saying no, we tell a big-ass story, keep delaying and stalling, look strained and constipated with our unspent *no*, but say we're "fine" while praying they figure out that we don't want to do it. It's why we don't consider being direct, or if we do, fear grips our sphincters.

What we effectively try to achieve is a tipping point with our people pleasing where it's like we've done so much gooding, efforting, avoiding, saving, and suffering that we finally hit our big payday. People feel so pleased, guilty, or obliged that they finally reward us with what we need, want, and expect.

We often see hinting as a requirement of navigating this world, especially when, depending on how we've been socialized and conditioned, we may have learned that speaking up for ourselves and being direct is rude or aggressive or unladylike or some other bullshit. So we've learned communication styles that fit around our roles without realizing how passive our communication is and how it waters down or erases our *no* even when we deign to express it.

But we're not merely hinting as part of our communication pattern: We're also doing it as part of avoiding conflict and criticism while simultaneously quietly (or so we think) expressing our hurt, frustration, and resentment.

All humans engage in passive-aggressive behavior. Don't side-eye me—it's true! Any time we say that we're "fine" or "okay" but then we make a face, act moody, continue complaining, send curt messages, bang the vacuum cleaner around the house sighing in the hope that our families will get off their asses and help tidy up (cough), this is passive aggression.

The Age of Obedience taught us to wear masks, so of course we're passive-aggressive. We've learned to project compliance while disguising our real feelings and become practiced at not matching what we do outwardly with how we truly feel inwardly.

Passive aggression is our masking our hidden feelings of resentment, hurt, and frustration and then subtly and not-so-subtly voicing them with obstructionist, resistant, and conflicting behavior while also denying we're doing it if we're called out on it, possibly while pointing out our good deeds at the same time.

Whichever way we drop hints, when people don't respond as we hoped, it reinforces the idea that there's no point in being honest or that boundaries are wrong. Cutting back on hinting is crucial because it creates clearer and more boundaried communication, and we stop expecting people to be mind readers or thinking that we can bend them to our will.

THE LANDMARKS OF BOUNDARIED COMMUNICATION

Am I doing boundaries right? Is this an okay boundary for me to have? Did I say/do the right thing? When trying to figure out how to say no and be clearer about what we're saying yes to in the process, anxiety about whether we're getting boundaries "right" and miscommunication can hold us back. A landmark is an easily distinguishable feature that lets us know where we are. You can cut back on hinting and also feel more secure in the boundaries you're creating and your *no* by using these landmarks of boundaried communication to guide you.

Compassion. This is a full-circle gig: We're not being that compassionate if we don't include ourselves in our compassion. It takes vulnerability, empathy, and kindness. When we create our boundaries with compassion, we acknowledge our humanness as well as that of others and recognize the need to do right by the situation or relationship. Compassion stops us from disregarding our feelings about something and then using our over-logical minds to convince ourselves that we are the problem.

Congruency. This is about our being in agreement with who we say we are, what we're trying to communicate, and our intentions so that we reduce the mixed messages to ourselves and others. The more we do this, the more successful outcomes we enjoy. It's recognizing where we're inwardly disagreeing, balking, and smarting while appearing to be outwardly compliant, or expecting others to be and do what we're not willing to do for ourselves. We must be what we seek.

Clarity. Rather than avoiding going all the way and relying on others to figure out what we mean, we strive to be clearer and more direct, both verbally and in actions, and when we realize that we haven't been clear, we evolve it next time 'around. Clarity requires vulnerability and taking responsibility for our feelings, so we also need to be prepared to ask questions as needed rather than being ambiguous or burying our heads in the sand. When you express what does and doesn't work for you, you've got to communicate how you feel and how their behavior affects you (we often omit this bit) through how you show up.

Ownership. It's communicating from a place of being a grown-up, which means being aware of our responsibilities. We've got to pay attention to ourselves instead of denying our feelings or continuing to engage without boundaries and trying to get people to change so that we can feel better about what we're doing. It's ensuring that what we express or state about someone is based on knowledge, not projecting the past or own feelings and thoughts, and that we also use "I" statements instead of shifting the focus to others.

Grace. This means expressing our feelings, beliefs, and ideas as well as expressing the truth (or our truths) with respect. It's seeing boundaries as a way to grow a relationship, not as a means of ruling others. Using the twofold approach ensures that we stay in our own lanes and that we don't inadvertently (or intentionally) engage in attention seeking or villainizing others by automatically assuming that they will do us harm if we say no.

TIDY UP YOUR *NO*S

Now that we've established that *no* isn't a dirty word, it's crucial to recognize that there are two types of *no*.

> A "hard" *no* is a straight-up *no*, and a "soft" *no* is anything that might be perceived as an indirect *no* or using language to try to let the other person down gently.

Typically clear and concise, a hard *no* can be discomforting, not because it's "bad," but because it cuts to the chase and keeps it real, something that might surprise the recipient because they might expect bullshitting or sucking up. It's the one you often need to use but fear or avoid because you don't want to seem harsh/rude/difficult/selfish/mean/cold/not a team player and all the other judgments you've leveled at yourself when you're emotionally blackmailing and second-guessing your way into doing stuff. Hard does not equal "harsh," but it might sound punitive, abrupt, or hostile if it's expressed in exasperation after excessive use of *yes* or soft *no*s.

While a soft *no* isn't necessarily long-winded, it tends to be accompanied by a level of detail or padding because, consciously or not, you feel as if you need to back up the *no*. This is fine *as long as* you're assertive instead of guilty. Each leads to different outcomes. Think of a soft *no* as what you might use for people you know well enough to feel assured that they'll respect it immediately. It's also, however, what you will use when you're fearful of being assertive with someone (or in general).

You might also use soft *no*s as a time-buying tactic that allows you to work up the courage (hopefully) to say no and/or to figure out an excuse.

They can sometimes be like halfway *no*s, where you kinda sorta say no but you tell the person that you'll think about it or to call you back (when you might not answer the phone). The more wishy-washy or detailed your *no*, the more it sounds like a *maybe*. Or, it sounds shady.

Use a hard *no* when . . .

- The situation or person requires clarity and conciseness. Do people need your life story or the breakdown of your schedule?
- The person likes it straight, with no chaser, or would hate to feel that their request made you feel guilty or shitty.
- You have experience with giving soft *no*s on that particular ask or subject and already know the impact on your well-being and want to spare yourself the stress.
- The ask is inappropriate and unreasonable, or you've already given a soft *no* and they're still pushing it. A soft *no* (or people pleasing) would only provide temporary relief from anxiety and delay the inevitable *no*.

Use a soft *no* with partners, friends, family, coworkers, and the like who consistently respect your boundaries, or where you would be prepared to switch to a hard *no* if it became clear it was required.

- You might opt for a soft *no* because you want to buffer the *no* with enough detail that the person will still continue to hold you in high esteem or so that the *no* doesn't endanger the relationship or the future prospects of getting something. No shade here. We all do it! Knowing your intentions, your "why," is important because if what follows doesn't reflect your boundaries, you will need to evolve your *no* so that it's clearer.
- If you're still talking past three or four sentences, your *no* isn't just soft. It's flaccid. Pause for breath. Notice the person you're saying no to.
- If it's taking you ages to compose and rewrite what might be a two-line response, your *no* is soft. You're anxious about something or trying to control how you're perceived.

- If you can say your soft *no* in fewer sentences, say it in fewer sentences. People don't need or want the filler.
- Where soft *no*s are misused and misconstrued is when they're padded with so much detail, excuses, apologies, justifications, and even drama that it obscures genuine reasons and your boundaries. Know your intentions. Are you trying to make the person regret asking so they don't do it again? Question your integrity, or your language and behavior may signal that you feel guilty and are open to negotiation. The latter causes shady folk to nearly rub their hands together in glee at the opportunity.
- If you are not intentional and boundaried with soft *no*s and instead rely on them to control how others perceive you, they have the opposite effect, so if you want to find joy in saying no or the aftereffects of it, be intentional in your choice of *no* where you can.

If you still feel uncomfortable with a hard *no*, try sandwiching a soft *no* between two hard *no*s. For instance, you can say, "Thanks for thinking of me, but I won't be able to attend. I've got a pretty packed schedule at the moment, so I'm saving my free time. I appreciate the invitation, and I hope it goes well, but I won't be able to make it."

What you discover when you incorporate some hard *no*s into your vocabulary is that plenty will accept them, so you will save yourself a lot of overthinking and long-winded or awkward conversations. It will also spare you from avoiding your phone or hiding behind pillars because you're dreading being asked again. In instances where more questions are asked, you can then add soft-*no* detail.

Instead of seeing *no* as letting someone down (and then endeavoring to let them down gently, not "hard"), treat all *no*s as respecting people enough to let them know where they stand.

"WHAT DID YOU MEAN BY THAT?"

These six magic words are an assertive reality check that lets you acknowledge your discomfort or uncertainty about something and gain clarity. *What did you mean when you said [repeat what they said as close to verbatim as possible]? What did you mean when you [insert a brief factual description of the thing they did]?* In intimate relationships you treasure, asking this question stops you from jumping to conclusions and fosters greater intimacy. Repeating what someone said or describing their behavior helps them see reality and how they're perceived, not how they think it came across in their imagination. It also means that someone who relies on people not being assertive and querying what might be their shady behavior has to acknowledge what they said or did or clarify what they meant.

FACTS DEAL WITH TRICKY PEOPLE

No matter if you hint, spray-paint it, or say it clearly and "nicely," there are some people in your life who are not interested in holding up their side of a healthy dynamic with you by addressing their own behavior. The trap that oh-so-many people fall into is they keep trying to appeal to this person's emotional side and their conscience, not realizing that this exposes them to further harm and is the equivalent of putting their bucket down an empty well and wondering why it comes up empty. Stop the madness, and stick to facts.

To the shady and narcissistically inclined, facts are like garlic and daylight to vampires. Use the be-factual approach to make you less vulnerable to gaslighting but also to help you recognize when they're bullying and pulling their coercive and abusive tactics. Only deal in facts.

- You said . . .
- You did . . . (factually describe what they did).
- Describe the problem and connect it with the impact or consequence.
- Mention dates.
- Follow up on things they've agreed to by putting it in an email.
- When they attempt to derail the conversation into a side disagreement, bringing up old stuff, or switching things around, don't buy in—stick to the facts.

Here are a few example statements:

- "When you shout at me and call me names, not only is this a really inappropriate means of making a point, but I also feel demoralized and upset." You could also add, "A relationship with mutual respect is very important to me. Much as I love and care for you, I will not be able to continue in this relationship if you're going to shout at me and name-call each time we have a disagreement."
- "We agreed to meet at seven thirty, not at eight thirty, and it means I'm going to have less time because I've already made an arrangement for ten."
- "When you arrive late, I'm left waiting around, and it's very frustrating."
- "You said that you were going to call at three, and now it's four. It'll have to be a quick call, as I've got a meeting." And then move on from it.
- "I'm questioning how serious you are because you went back on what you said and what we agreed to."

Other tips include these:

- Avoid saying, "You always" or "You never" because they will seize on this and immediately blow a hole in your argument by making up something or mentioning that time back in 1982 when they think they did something that disproves your claim.
- Although you're understandably upset by their actions, if you focus only on that and don't start off with the facts, they'll dispute your

assessment of things or switch it around to their being upset with you about your comments. For instance, "You make me feel so inadequate. Why am I not good enough for you? What did I do wrong?" doesn't express "You've lied to me about XYZ, and you're taking pure liberties by doing ABC."

When you stick to facts with people who hate facts, they become aware of your boundaries and realize that they can't eff with you.

It's not that you need to become emotionless, but you need to stop acting as if you're coming from the same level of awareness or that you both want the same things.

BROKEN RECORD

As a people pleaser, it can be excruciating when people don't take us at our first or even fifth *no*s, and this can wear us down and have us saying *yes* to get them off of our backs. Of course, this type of *yes* only causes us pain and problems. With the "broken record" strategy, a common assertiveness technique, you communicate in a way that stands behind you by being more persistent in a calm, respectful way that reinforces your point.

The aim is to clearly state whatever it is that you need to say in as calm and relaxed a manner as possible. The end goal is that they listen, accept your answer, and back away.

Consider the following example conversation:

Coworker: Ugh, I need some help on this project [and proceeds to go into an explanation where you realize that it's too much for you to take on].

You: I understand that you're stuck, but based on everything that you're looking to get done, I won't be able to help out this time.

Coworker: I know it sounds like a lot, but you're so bright and superfast at stuff that I'm sure it wouldn't be too much for you.

We'll have fun together, and I'm sure it will look good to [the boss]. Come on, please?

You: Thanks, but really, I can't. I've got a lot on my plate and there's no way that I'd be able to do all that stuff too. I don't want to overstretch myself and end up letting you or one of my other projects down.

Coworker: I can't imagine that you would ever be in that situation. I'm sure it will be fine.

You: I guess I'm not being clear enough, but really, I can't take it on.

At this point, you can suggest an alternative person, or you could say, "As I said, there's no way I'll be able to take that on, and I appreciate your having such faith in my capabilities, but if you're still stuck once I've completed my own deadline, I could help you out with _____ and _____ [specific elements of the project as opposed to all of it]."

If the request is coming from a respectful source and is something that, with further discussion, could respect each of your needs and expectations, then you can potentially find a solution you can both live with.

You might, understandably, feel nervous, especially if you're not used to saying no or the person is wheedling, persistent, or even petulant. As you repeat and evolve the stating of your position, the nervousness often dissipates, not least because by being in the present, you're aware of what's going on and how the person not respecting your *no* is acting from their baggage, not based on the validity of your *no*. You recognize that regardless of what they say or do, your answer is still that you cannot meet their request because of your recognition of your boundaries.

EMBRACE HEALTHY BOUNDARIES

- Have realistic expectations of your *no*. Your boundaries are for you first and foremost, not about trying to rule others. No matter how valid your *no*, no matter how nicely you say it, people will not always respond how you would like. They don't have to respond "well," and if they don't, it has more to do with their baggage as well as possibly not being used to hearing *no* from you.

- Sometimes you will have to say no more than once, even though, in theory, people should know when they're expecting too much or are out of line. But they don't because they're humans, and even if they do, these are your boundaries, so you need to communicate what does and doesn't work for you.

- Prep for success, not failure. Don't go in all guns blazing or acting and thinking as if you're going to get run over. Remind yourself that it's more than okay to say no and that it's about having a stake in your life, not always getting things to go your way.

- Take some deep breaths if needed. Some people find it useful to count up to ten and then back down to one to steady themselves.

- Don't focus on letting people down gently because it's where you get your pleaser involved and try to take responsibility for their feelings and behavior. It also reinforces an underlying belief that *no* hurts people's feelings. It doesn't—dynamics do.

- Most people, even if they don't realize it until the benefit of hindsight, like to know where they stand. The only people who don't are the ones who capitalize on your not knowing where *you* stand.

TROUBLESHOOTING *NO*

I've realized that something isn't working for me, but I don't feel ready to tell the person or deal with their feelings about it. What do I say if they ask me if something's wrong?

I empathize, and there's every possibility that with time, you will feel more ready. That space can feel like a boundary you need to uphold. But don't wait to feel 100 percent ready because most humans, unless they're the type who'd have a fight with a paper bag, aren't in a rush to risk conflict or criticism. Here's the key: At the point where the person asks, don't deny it* because that's gaslighting, something all humans are guilty of at times. When you deny another person's reality, you cause them to second-guess and doubt themselves, so don't tell them everything is okay when, for instance, you've been ignoring their texts and calls or are about to end the relationship. But that doesn't mean you have to spill your guts. "You're right. I have been [acknowledge what they've noticed]. I'm going through some stuff at the moment and need time to figure that out. Can we catch up next week?" Or, if you already know and are trying to avoid confrontation, express as best as you can what's going on.

I dropped the hinting and came out straight with what was bothering me, and nothing's changed. What does this mean?

Well done for speaking up. I know it must have been uncomfortable. The fact that you haven't seen an immediate change doesn't mean that it was a waste of time to speak up. You showed up. You're endeavoring to be more honest. Keep going. It's absolutely okay to let someone know when something doesn't work for you, but it doesn't mean that they're going to feel duty bound or in a position to change it. They're coming from a different level of awareness and may not see their intent and actions with the same eyes that you do. Rather than making the primary focus getting them to change and amend their behavior so that you feel better, get on with doing what you need to do for yourself so that you feel better. This will give you a clearer sense of how you want to proceed and allows you to own your side of the boundary. Make sure that when you communicate what's bothering you that you also, where you can, express what needs to change or what it is that you need or want. Often, people leave that bit out.

I tend to feel confused when I know that I need to say no. What's going on here?

---

* If this person is abusive and you fear for your safety, there is a legit reason to not say something so that you can safely extricate yourself from the situation without their becoming violent or turning on the charm to wheedle you into staying.

Many people pleasers have a pattern of feeling confused in situations where they need, want to, or should say no. It's not only part of their fight-flight-freeze response, but it's also their habit of labeling the feelings that come up in these contexts. What we need to pay attention to is where we've gotten into the habit of saying we're confused as a strategy for avoiding our feelings of discomfort or the truth about what the other person is doing.

I love this person, but they really disappointed me. We've talked it through, but it keeps resurfacing when they say or do something that makes me think they still don't get it. What am I missing here?

It keeps coming up because even though you've clearly expressed some or even a lot of your upset, there is something you've avoided explicitly saying for fear of hurting their feelings or negative consequences. There's something you've danced around, or it isn't clear what it is that you need or want to happen next. And then you're resentful and annoyed when you feel as if you spared them and that they're still being insensitive. Say the thing that needs to be said so that both of you get it. Allowing for the possibility of conflict is part of intimacy. It's not that you need to disagree all the time, but you need to know that when you need to, you can and will. Allow yourself to be seen and heard so that you can come out the other side of this experience.

My parent keeps going on about my not being married yet and wanting grandchildren every time we speak, and they haven't stopped even though it's blatantly making me uncomfortable. What can I say to them?

A sample script might go as follows: "When we talk and your primary focus is [asking why I'm not in a relationship or married yet, or when I'm going to give you a grandchild, or comparing me to your friends' adult children], it gives me this sense that you are not interested in me and that I'm disappointing and failing you. That's not a nice feeling, and I also don't like dreading your calls or feeling nervous about spending time with you and that I'm going to have to defend who I am. Even if it's not what you intended, I need you to stop trying to make me feel bad about myself to get me to be who you want me to be. Otherwise, it will impact our relationship, and I'm going to feel resentful. I value our relationship and want to feel as if [I can enjoy spending time with you], and that's why I'm telling you this."

My parent keeps complaining about my sibling to me or expecting me to take sides. What should I do?

It's bad boundaries for parents to interfere with and manipulate the relationships between siblings. It creates guilt, shame, and division. Your parent needs to find someone else to bitch to, especially when they want you to take sides or it interferes with your relationship with your sibling. Siblings have the right to moan to one another about their parents, but parents, given their authority and position, cannot do that with their children, even adult ones. You can also say: "Mom/Dad, I appreciate that things are difficult between you and [sibling], but I can't be involved in this." Try the broken record strategy by saying, "I don't want to discuss/ be involved in this." Remember, other people have baggage too, and often the reason why a parent is doing this, aside from it being a habit, is that it happened in their own family dynamic.

Aren't I inviting more conflict into my life by being more direct?

Associating directness with conflict comes from our social conditioning. It causes us to shut off our feelings and fear being disobedient, so we have a low tolerance for discomfort around potential conflict and criticism. This creates unrealistic expectations of saying yes *and* no. If you're always indirect or saying yes even when you mean *no*, you'll be in constant conflict with yourself internally, and you will also invite more pain and problems. Why pretend to be keeping the peace when you're silently waging war with yourself?

13

LEARN FROM ERUPTIONS
AND CHALLENGES

When I share stories from this seventeen-year (and counting) period of my life where I've been reclaiming myself from the cycle of people pleasing, people often mistakenly perceive my meeting my now husband in those first eight months and going on to have two children as my happy ending. These assumptions cater to a common misconception that we simply need to do some self-work or announce our boundaries, and then when we get what we want, job done.

What I learned and did in those first eight months was like taking an accelerated overview class and my thinking, *Hmmm, so it turns out that I can do this stuff and I've had a taste of how much better I and my life can feel. I don't know what lies ahead, but I'm going to commit to the lifelong, in-depth course and see where it takes me.*

And where it's taken me is to experiencing so much joy *and also* being tested to what has felt like the absolute max at times.

Motherhood and being a partner brought me face-to-face with how I often automatically (and unnecessarily) deferred my needs and didn't ask for help enough, among many other things. Self-employment shone a megawatt light on my perfectionism and people pleasing, forcing me to set limits with myself in particular and to confront my fear of rejection and failure.

But there *is* a watershed moment in this journey that marked the start of several years of what felt like a road of trials: the wedding and the eventual decision to have both my father and stepfather walk me down the aisle.

As beautiful as that day was, it marked the end of a pretense that my father's absence and abandonment had not devastated me, us. It took a few months before I registered that my father and most of that side had distanced themselves from me, and it unleashed deeply buried grief and anger that I spent the next four years of that silence addressing with various therapies and through the day-to-day of living my life and dealing with other eruptions and challenges that came my way.

I'd feel as if I was getting on a more even keel, and then something else would come along, like the clash with my mother-in-law and getting the silent treatment from my mother for up to a year at a time when my boundaries didn't fit her expectations. Or there's when one of my brothers and my brother-in-law were seriously ill at the same time while dealing with a racist landlord in between selling one home and buying another. It was pushing myself to achieve more and feeling unrecognized and, at times, having such bad tinnitus (when you hear sounds even though you're not hearing something externally) and feeling so frustrated with it and myself about why I couldn't make it go away that I became depressed. There's receiving the call from my stepmother about my father's cancer, reconnecting with him, and then holding his hand as he died ten months later with the biggest grin on his face. It was taking a couple of months off after his passing and trying to get back to "normal," only to find that I didn't have enough bandwidth to do everything I used to, and so having to slow right down, do a lot less, and go through more than two years of feeling "lost" only to stumble into more joy along the way. And so it continues.

There are oh-so-common traps that we can fall into on our recovery journeys, including the following:

- Expecting to have to say no to something only once.
- Expecting to put a concerted effort into boundaries for a few months or through a difficult period and that this should take care of us for all time without further consistent boundaries.
- Expecting people to roll over and be grateful that we've finally spoken up after holding back or for pointing out something instead of recognizing that they will experience discomfort and react from wherever they are with their own emotional baggage.
- Not expecting pushback if we said or asked it nicely or our boundary is valid.
- Believing that because we've done this self-work that we shouldn't come up against old problems and challenges or that these should be easier, and then feeling like a failure or disillusioned with boundaries.
- Overstepping boundaries by expecting people to have changed and to be willing to be more boundaried because of what we're doing.
- Thinking we have everything under control and then feeling wounded when something happens despite our better boundaries.
- Not expecting people to say no.

Even though you may have done your absolute best to be a Good Person or even though you've started to say no, you are going to experience challenges and, sometimes, eruptions. And whether it's during these events or in the aftermath, or even in the months or years that follow, you're going to learn from these challenges, sometimes willingly and at other times with gritted teeth or kicking and screaming as you try to hold on to wanting to be right or how things used to be.

You're sometimes going to make what might be a split-second decision to take a shortcut to get or avoid something. And you might even forget that you made that decision, but your boundaries don't, and so it might come back to you in some way. This isn't because you're being punished. Our actions and intentions, both the conscious and unconscious ones, have consequences. As I've previously said, how we do something is how we do a lot of things. It's a metaphor for how we approach life. If we tend to skip our own basic needs, such as going to the bathroom, regular meals, sleep, and rest, it's because we skip ourselves. When we experience eruptions and challenges, we're forced to take a bit more care, to stop skipping the small stuff that can lead up to the big stuff.

LEARN FROM ERUPTIONS AND CHALLENGES BY PEOPLE-PLEASER STYLE

Gooders will have to confront the limitations of their image and learn to be okay with not always being liked or right.

Efforters will have to confront the limitations of their bandwidth and learn to be okay with doing less.

Avoiders will have to confront the limitations of always deferring themselves and learn to be okay with discomforting themselves and others.

Savers will have to confront the limitations of disowning themselves to be there for others and will have to learn to be okay with putting themselves first.

Sufferers will have to confront the limitations of relying on being victimized as an identity and learn to be okay with allowing themselves to be happy.

NAVIGATING AND PROCESSING ERUPTIONS

Suppressing and repressing yourself is like being a pressure cooker that's been left on for too long. All your unexpressed feelings, your anger over your old hurts and losses, gets turned inward or onto someone else or even a group of people, which is highly corrosive to your well-being and your intimate relationships.

Eruptions—where you or your life *implode*, so you go through an internal crisis and your body stops you in your tracks or everything in your life seems to collapse at once or in a relatively short period, or where you *explode*, so you unleash or behave uncharacteristically—occur because you've maxed out after suppressing and repressing your needs, desires, expectations, feelings, and opinions. You can no longer hold it in, and the eruption is a hard stop where you've struggled to pause or slow down.

The eruption is the outcome of running too many red lights. Your body, your life, tries to warn you in subtle ways at first and then gradually ups the ante to try to get your attention. And if you keep ignoring yourself, you get the eruption. You crash.

This is similar to our experiences of pain and illness, something I came to understand from having had a chronic illness (sarcoidosis) and then grappling with tinnitus for several years. My five-element acupuncturist and wonderful sage and mentor, the late Silvio Andrade, explained during one of those times I was, yet again, weeping on him feeling frustrated with my body, that where we experience pain or illness isn't necessarily where it started and is in response to imbalances in the body. Before we felt the pain, obviously outside of an injury, or we became unwell, our bodies gave smaller signs and warnings that something was wrong; it's that we may have been so busy, so caught up in other people's business that we didn't notice or ignored it.

Like when I found a hard lump in my finger in the summer of 2003 and pushed it to the back of my mind because I'd broken off my engagement, started a new job, and was now embroiled in an affair with a co-worker who had a girlfriend. After a lifetime of buried emotional stress that had manifested in various other illnesses, this particular symptom signaled how far in crisis my immune system was. A few months later, I could barely see out of one eye and kept going along with doctors who dismissed me, and then it eventually got so bad that I wound up in the hospital, and tests and X-rays showed how I was riddled with lumps and other symptoms. And you'd think all of that would be enough, but several months later, I had an appalling panic attack on one of the busiest streets in Central London one Friday night. The man I was having an affair with was harassing me about male colleagues talking to me, and the experience and aftereffects were so traumatic that just being around him set off panic in me, leaving me with no choice but to keep my distance. The body called, I did not listen, and so it forced me—again and again, I might add.

The mistake many make when they erupt is blaming and shaming themselves. Whether it's about no longer being able to emotionally, mentally, and physically cope with their lives and experiencing depression or a breakdown; whether it's no longer being able to meet other people's expectations and feeling as though they're letting everyone down and being a burden or a failure; whether it's how they behaved toward others or expressed their anger, they feel as though whatever's happening is proof that boundaries are wrong, that people cannot handle assertiveness, and that their bodies are failing them. They then continue beating themselves up, holding themselves back from accessing the support they need or letting themselves rest and recover, and they retreat into themselves. And so the people-pleasing cycle continues.

Even if some appear to get over what happened because they regard the eruption as a failure or a source of shame, they fear the eruption happening again. They feel as if they have to stick rigidly to whatever self-care routine they put in place, fearing that if they miss a day or an item, it will fast-track them back to Eruption Central. Or they tiptoe around themselves and others, being fearful of their *no* and overthinking and catastrophizing. They might become afraid of wanting something or exposing themselves to getting hurt in case they can't cope with it, so they avoid relationships or take a job where they don't feel too stretched. And this is fine for a time because it might be exactly what they need, but when it becomes a form of purgatory for the old eruption and hiding out, this is unhealthy.

Although you might experience shame—that sense of being a Bad Person and that what you're feeling, thinking, doing, or experiencing means you're not worthy of connection, meeting your needs, or having a different perspective—don't take up residence there. Don't feed it. Even if you don't feel in a position to do much for yourself, go back to step 2 (page 123) and ask yourself, *What's the baggage behind this?* And then ask, *What is it that I need?* and see what pops into your head. From there, you will be able to gradually figure out how to authentically meet this need, whether it's literally doing this for yourself, voicing that need to a safe person, or allowing yourself to access resources and support.

This eruption, as horrible as it might feel in the midst of it, is helping you feel more alive. You might not fit back into your old life and may find it difficult to do all the things you did previously. Don't panic. Give yourself time. But also recognize that maybe you didn't have to be doing all the things, and give yourself a chance to discover who you might become if you gave yourself permission to do less and to receive help, support, and intimacy.

You've got to feel to heal, and when you don't let yourself feel, you erupt. So take the eruption and use it to reconnect with yourself, to regain and reclaim your *no*, so that you can reclaim yourself.

Here are some questions to help you figure out what's going on:

- What can I say no to right now that will give me the bandwidth to be here for myself and limit further negative impact from [whatever happened or is occurring]? Now that I'm going through this, what is it that I need to stop or put on pause while I get a handle on things?
- Where have I gone way past my limits and way over my bandwidth trying to be all things to all people?
- With the benefit of hindsight and acknowledging what I'm experiencing, where have I exploited myself (or allowed others to)?
- Where have I clung to an identity, a role, or a painful or unfulfilling relationship or situation because I'm scared of my potential and who I could be?

- Where am I hating on myself for not being my perfect, idealized self, and how can I be even a little bit kinder toward myself and recognize my humanness?
- What have I been doing to anesthetize myself against the effects of my people pleasing and to avoid saying no (e.g., drinking, eating your feelings, exercising too much, overworking, shopping, gambling, collecting attention on dating apps, hooking up)? And what is this telling me that I need?
- Where is it that I don't like the consequences of an old *yes* and so I'm bearing a grudge against myself, possibly because I feel powerless about the other person or feel I failed, and how can I step away from blame and move to responsibility?

> Acknowledge your grief, and rather than shove it back down or judge yourself, sit alongside it. Allow yourself to get support and develop practices because being cracked open can feel like being naked in the cold. You will have to prioritize yourself and let people help you, which will involve being the "burden" you fear so that you can shed the old role and stop pretending you don't have needs.

Eruptions bring ungrieved grief, unprocessed emotional baggage, to the forefront by surfacing your old pain, fear, and guilt in such a way that you don't have any choice but to confront it. Although it's unwanted and can be incredibly uncomfortable and painful, the eruption cracks you wide-open and forces you to unpack, declutter, and tidy up some of your emotional baggage so that you can regain some of your bandwidth and reclaim yourself.

Anger is a valid emotion that alerts you to where you've experienced an injustice (or where you feel that you have). Sometimes that injustice will be other people's actions, and sometimes it's what you've done to yourself. It takes many forms, including irritation, frustration, and victimization, and also contained within it is fear, your sense of being under threat that galvanizes you to protect yourself by fighting, fleeing, or freezing.

Many humans are socialized to be ashamed, not only of anger, but of their feelings full stop. Anger is often associated with badness or its most heightened version, rage, which we imagine as violence toward an environment or another person. Our people pleasing, though, is the silent rage of our buried selves that we manage to keep under control until we can't.

But anger is a valid and necessary emotion. It's one of many you experience, with none being more important or acceptable than the other. They're simply emotions. All have useful intel alerting you to your inner state and what's potentially happening around you so that you can decipher what you need—hence emotional intelligence.

Your feelings, if you consistently feel them, help you recognize other people's and your own feelings, to orient and push yourself to take action, and to understand what's going on.

People pleasing numbs your feelings. If you imagine all your feelings as one of those old telephone switchboards, you behave as if you can cherry-pick the palatable, socially acceptable, and instant-gratification feelings and ignore the rest. But people pleasing and all the avoidance that comes with it is the equivalent of flicking the master switch to turn them all off.

If you've turned down (numbed) or turned off (deadened) your feelings, you can't feel your boundaries, so you cannot sense and respond to your needs nor have a real honest connection and assessment of your desires, expectations, and thoughts. On those occasions when you recognize feelings even if you don't know what they are, they're often heightened, which can cause you to hastily shut them down or attach an incorrect meaning and story to them. It's as if they can't believe they're getting an airing and come rushing up. You will also unconsciously do things to temporarily feel alive that can prove to be self-destructive and exacerbate or create challenges.

Feelings are also the path to interdependence, where you are healthily independent but also able to depend on others without losing yourself, as opposed to codependency where you don't know where you end and others begin or are so afraid of getting hurt that you cut yourself off.

You've thought that you can skip vulnerability by avoiding feeling too much and being and doing what you can to limit or outright avoid conflict, criticism, disappointment, loss, and rejection. But avoiding these is to avoid life. They're life's inevitables. It's not that we experience these all the time, but we *are* supposed to experience them, and without them, we cannot and will not experience joy. *To allow ourselves to experience joy is to be willing to say and receive no; it is to be present to life.*

> Where you can, give yourself more time to recover from an eruption than you're comfortable with. You'll thank yourself for it when you don't find yourself back in your normal routine and realizing that you were not ready yet.

NAVIGATING AND PROCESSING CHALLENGES

As a recovering people pleaser used to associating what happens with something you did or didn't do or wanting things to be all smooth sailing, you will be self-critical when challenges arise, thinking they're unfair and unwarranted. A part of you will be like, *It's. Not. Fair. I did all the things. I'm a good person. I haven't done anything wrong. I can't believe they said or did that thing even though I . . .* Quite frankly, sometimes a challenge will wear down your last nerve and make you want to scream at being out of control or having more control than you'd like in that moment.

> Challenges are situations, wanted *and* unwanted, that test your character, habits of thinking and behavior, and your bandwidth.

Challenges, as frustrating, annoying, and downright discomforting as they might be, are opportunities to level up your boundaries in some way and to take care of yourself.

You will, as you become attuned to challenges showing up in your life, stop taking them quite so personally and dig a bit deeper into owning yourself. Through challenges, you will confront what you didn't even know needed confronting or that you didn't realize you were avoiding, and so you will heal, grow, and learn in some way, even if you don't recognize this until you're further down the road and looking back. You will, as a result of challenges, identify things you need to be, do, say, or have, and you will figure it out as you go along.

It's crucial to acknowledge, though, that even though, as a result of something you're going through, you will say *no*s in ways that bring you closer to yourself, sometimes a challenge is a life event or set of events that call on you to feel your feelings and grieve. Yes, we do often recognize how something is, was, a blessing in disguise. But sometimes, even though we might be more ourselves in ways we didn't imagine, whatever happened sucks. And it's okay to call it.

I wholeheartedly believe in gratitude, that appreciation of what you have and recognizing how something unwanted has also given you something you do want or that you do appreciate, sometimes with gritted teeth. But if something sucky happens and you're quick to be like, *This is a blessing in disguise. I'm, like, so grateful*, you're bypassing your very real experience and emotions. Sure, you may well be grateful further down the line, but first you've got to be pissed off. You've got to gradually allow yourself to experience the myriad of emotions.

If you look at the scales of emotions, you can't skip from rage straight to joy.[1] Along the way as you feel your feelings and sometimes try to shove them back down and then feel again, and as you say no *and* yes, you will experience doubt, worry, overwhelm, frustration, boredom, hopefulness, and enthusiasm, among other feelings. You can and will dig yourself out, but give yourself time.

It's okay to find challenges difficult. They can be very triggering, and sometimes it feels like it's one thing after another and you want to lie down and curl into a ball and wait for it all to pass. You might struggle with not knowing all the steps or what's next; you might hate not having a plan or knowing what your path is and find yourself looking to anything and anyone to tell you what to do. It's like, *What if I'm saying yes or no to the wrong thing? How am I supposed to know what I'm supposed to say no to if I don't even know what the hell I want?*

News flash: You're not supposed to always know what you want, not least because of socialization and conditioning. You've been programmed to want certain things even when they haven't been a fit, and what you were taught was available to you reflects a much earlier stage of your life. This is why so many people struggle with realizing that their job, career, business, what they thought was the Path, is not for them. They often look to another structure, another box to fit into because, especially if you were born before the nineties, you heard a lot about climbing the ladder and getting a good, stable job. Much like how when people say they want to leave their relationships and their friends ask, "Are they beating you? They cheating on you?" there was an attitude that you should stay in situations for whatever small benefits they may offer or unless something really bad happens.

We've also been conditioned to believe that we're supposed to work ourselves to the bone until retirement and *then* we get to say no to certain things and enjoy our lives. What we don't consider is that after living and working as if we're machines and catering to everyone else, we might not have the health or energy to enjoy our lives. How about we be even a little bit more intentional and boundaried and start enjoying our lives now?

How we see the problem is the problem and the challenge. We think that we're not supposed to be experiencing a problem in that specific instance and/or that given who we are and what we think we've done, that we shouldn't be. Challenges, including problems, are there to let us know where there's a flaw in our thinking, attitude, or actions, but also to help us grow some more. I know it's annoying sometimes. We want to be left alone and not have to stretch again. And we can dodge it, but eventually we have to discern our *no* so that we can open up to our happy *yes*.

Here are some questions to help you figure out what's going on:

- What is this challenge a metaphor for? Where else have I felt, thought, and acted similarly? Does how I've handled this particular thing speak for how I handle other things?
- What am I trying to get or avoid? What role am I playing in this dynamic?
- Where am I avoiding being direct and trying to off-load my responsibility to the other person?
- Where haven't I listened to myself? What have I denied, rationalized, minimized, and excused?
- Where did I go back on an old *no* because I was bored, lonely, horny, hungry, tired, *something*?
- Where have I based my expectations of myself or others on the picture I've painted in my mind instead of in reality? Where am I expecting people to think the same way or do things the way I do, even though they're not me?
- Who, despite my saying no, isn't getting it, and what does this mean? If applicable, where do I need to say hell no or a hell effing no?
- What, if anything, is this challenge showing me about where I've played it small and undervalued myself?
- Does what I've been doing in this instance reflect my actual self or an identity I'm trying to portray, and how is that causing problems for me?
- Do I want what I say I want, and if so, what will I have to say no to even though it might mean being very uncomfortable for a while and feeling unsure?
- What is the boundary that this challenge is telling me that I need to create?

> What do you need to let go of?
>
> What do you get to say yes to if you allow yourself to say no?

Remember: If you say no, you will forgive yourself and the situation by having better boundaries than before.

Repeat frustrations point to a process, personal rule, or something you can create or do that will make your life easier. These help you immediately communicate your boundaries, give a *no*, or manage your bandwidth. For example:

- Setting up a process at work or home that helps you stop being the bottleneck.
- An automatic email responder that communicates the hours you reply to email.
- Blocking out no-interruption time in your calendar.
- Setting up your phone to automatically go on Do Not Disturb each evening.
- A personal rule that you don't say yes to certain types of request or that you stop giving *yeses* once you notice a certain feeling.
- A document, video, or page on your website that explains the process and communicates expectations or what is or isn't available.

EMBRACE HEALTHY BOUNDARIES

- While eruptions can feel very unpleasant during and in the aftermath, they are our watershed moments. Things will have to change and we will be changed because of this, and so there will be grieving because we think how we were is the only way that we can be—but we are so much more.

- Disappointment is there to let you know what's possible so that you have healthier expectations, of yourself and others.

- Just by noticing people pleasing, you're noticing the warning flags of where you're going through yellow and red lights. By paying attention to where you are doing this, you can consciously intervene and make adjustments. You can ask: *What's going on with me? What's going on here?*

- There are trade-offs with everything, so the clearer you are on who you are and want to be, what matters to you, and how you want to feel and continue feeling, the easier it is to be okay with what you let go of because you understand what you gain.

- Recognizing that something isn't working and saying no isn't a failure, it's a success. The "failure" would be pretending it's not happening, continuing to try to get a return on investment, and making yourself suffer, effectively blocking yourself from getting what you need out of this situation and taking your newfound discernment somewhere new.

- The right decision doesn't always feel good immediately, especially when you're used to saying yes while ignoring how shitty you feel or how wrong it is. Be kind to yourself, and be careful of catastrophic thinking and the stories you tell yourself about how others will react or what your feelings mean.

- You will get pushback on your *no* sometimes, not because it's wrong but to refine the landmarks (compassion, congruency, clarity, grace, and ownership) and also to make sure you're serious about who you say you are and want to be. If you can say no and honor it only in perfect conditions where everyone acquiesces, you'll fold faster than a busted lawn chair the moment you get the slightest whiff of a shortcut, life's inevitables, or anxiety or stress.

- Create boundaries instead of building walls. It's all too easy to retreat into yourself and become guarded and defensive when you come against eruptions and challenges, but these are walls that defend against the past and it expresses where you haven't forgiven yourself yet. That's okay, but find the boundary, find the *no*, so you can move forward with love, care, trust, and respect instead of suspicion.

- There are plenty of people who don't use your vulnerabilities and, yes, your weaknesses against you, who feel uncomfortable with exploiting you because they are aware of their own limits. They see your discomfort with boundaries and still treat you with love, care, trust, and respect. Say no and allow yourself to have more boundaries so that you can forge and enjoy intimate relationships.

TROUBLESHOOTING *NO*

I've started saying no and now it feels like all I do is feel, and it's so uncomfortable and raw. Will it stay like this?

Buried emotions don't disappear; they wreak havoc. However, don't confuse the initial onslaught of feelings after avoiding them as being what feeling your feelings are like on the whole. Of course your emotions feel very acute when you've shoved them down. But they move on remarkably quickly when you allow yourself to feel and you stop feeling held hostage by them. These feelings you're wrestling with are not a permanent statement of the future. There will be a weather change, and they will shift and ebb and flow.

I really do want to move past a painful event with healthier boundaries, but I feel stuck thinking about what happened. What's going on?

If you're still feeling bad about something, it's because of the untrue stories you're telling yourself about what happened. Otherwise, those feelings would have evolved once you were being more truthful. If you're blaming and shaming yourself, if you're making something about your not being good enough, you're not being truthful with yourself yet. Be careful of treating failure or hurt as reflective of something unchangeable. You can only see the immediate stretch ahead of what is a much longer road, so be gentle with yourself.

I did something that reflects who I am instead of going along to get along, and people didn't like it. Surely this means I need to rethink what I'm doing?

Don't base your perception of the validity of *no* or your boundaries purely on how other people reacted because this can be hella misleading. If I'd based whether or not to say no and have boundaries on one response, I might not have bothered again and decided that people couldn't handle it and that it wasn't worth the headache. But I did say no again, and guess what? They either had no pushback, or even if they did, my *no* was still valid. Also, people can't take boundaries, including who you are, seriously, if you keep chopping and changing it. Keep showing up so they know whom and what to expect and can gradually adjust.

What do you do when you realize you could have done things differently?

Now that you have far greater understanding of yourself and recognize where you were scared or where you felt ill-equipped to handle conflict and other challenges, you might have regrets. You will experience grief about what you didn't know and who you could have been *if only* . . . You might not be where you thought you would be right now. It's okay to feel upset about that, but say no to losing yourself in it. Own what you've learned so that you can move forward with boundaries instead of more regrets about the same thing still coming back at you in different guises through new challenges. You were in a different place back then, and you can't know what you don't know. Your regret will lessen if you take good care of your younger self and show them compassion and empathy through the better choices and boundaries now and up ahead.

Someone in my life is looking for a second chance, and I'm not sure that I want to grant it but feel like I should, especially because I have better boundaries now.

Take the *should* out of this and acknowledge that you're not sure or don't want to. Also, acknowledge what, if anything, you hope to get in return or avoid if you go ahead. If this person doesn't have healthy boundaries and expects you to engage at your previous level of boundaries, it's only a matter of time until it's pain and problems. Your intention may be to give another chance, to show support, but the result is that this person will interpret this as a green light to re-create the same problem. Consciously or not, if you keep pursuing a do-over, you will keep getting the same undesired results because you're too focused on how you want yourself and others to look.

I said no to someone I don't normally say it to, and they cussed me out/ cut me off/tried to make me feel really shitty about myself. What the hell?

If someone flips their wig with you because you said no or because you prioritize taking care of your own boundaries and know your responsibilities, this is a sign that your *no* was overdue. The *yes* buffet is officially closed.

CONCLUSION

Where you won't say no (or don't realize you need to), life is going to make you say it anyway. It will do it for you through other people's boundaries or the culmination of various avoided decisions and *no*s that club together, typically at a highly inconvenient time, and force you to have to make changes.

It's as if life, or as I like to call it, Professor Life, looks at you and goes, *Hmm, how's [your name] getting on? Are they being more authentic? Well, lookee here. They've got this, this, and this going on where they won't say no even though they really need or want to. Okay, so how can we shake things up so that they can move toward claiming the life, the self, that's really theirs? What do we need to give [your name] to help them get this figured out so that they can learn enough to move forward and out of this pattern?* And if certain lessons come around again and again through challenges and you keep deferring or dodging them, those *no*s you've avoided erupt in some way.

> By receiving *no* from the things you wouldn't say no to, you're forced to finally say no so that you can also say yes.

Sometimes you will find yourself wrestling with *no* collectively, as we all have been with the pandemic. Humans needed to slow down, to look at how they were living their lives, to say no, but we always had something else to do. And then the pandemic happened, and suddenly, everything was upended as most of the world went into lockdown. It was a hard stop. A lot of us—even if we were, for all intents and purposes, okay in the sense of not having lost our jobs or our health or a loved one, and even enjoyed aspects of the slowdown—still found it difficult. For those of us who'd relied on the pace of our lives to avoid ourselves, to avoid our *nos*, we may not have had the gym, bar, work, or everybody else's stuff to escape to. And even if we weren't working from home, we may have been limited by the lockdown in terms of whom we could connect with or what we could do. Some of us, even though it may have taken a while to register, felt relief. We finally had an out from all of the *yes*es. In other instances, the pandemic made aspects of our lives so unlivable, so unsustainable, that we finally said no and stepped away from what wasn't working for us. The pandemic has forced us to confront our relationships with obedience and compliance, something we'll likely grapple with for some years to come.

You will learn where you need to say no from wanted and unwanted experiences—birth, death, loss, bullying and harassment, menopause, disability, children growing and then leaving the nest, starting a new relationship, engagement, marriage, breakups, illness, achievement and recognition, getting the long-hoped-for thing, a parent having to stay with you, becoming a caregiver for a sick relative, finally recognizing something about yourself after years of masking it, fallouts, failure and mistakes, doing something that with the benefit of hindsight you realize wasn't your best moment, joys beyond your wildest dreams, outgrowing relationships, body changes, moves, *life*.

Sometimes you will get what you thought you wanted and realize it's not for you, and will have to reconcile yourself with this knowledge and take action. And other times, you won't get something you definitely want in the form you expected it to be or at all, and it will be painful.

These events will clarify or reveal aspects of yourself. They might reveal unconscious biases that leave you feeling super uncomfortable at the discovery but also more awake. You will align with your preferences instead of old and obsolete programming.

People and situations that remind you of others from your past will invite you to see what you couldn't before even though you thought you'd seen and knew all the things. Life will present you with old *yes*es and old *no*s, even though you thought you were done and that that person or thing didn't bother you anymore. And that's not because you hadn't done the work but because these events are opportunities to grieve deeper, to grieve from new angles, to embrace joy. You haven't faced all possible situations, so how could you possibly be "done"?

If you say you don't like a particular thing or that something is a priority, Professor Life *will* present you with situations, *yes*es and *no*s, that put you to the test.

Professor Life isn't trying to catch you out and make a tit out of you; it's trying to help you. If you say that you are a certain type of person or that you need or want something, you will have to identify what you need to say no to that upholds that. Otherwise, what you say means jack. Your actions won't match your words, intentions, and how you truly feel inside. It's like when people tell me they're ready for a serious relationship, but then they're in a casual one being ambiguous about who they are and what they need and want while they people-please in the hope that the person will be like, *Aw, they've bent over backward and let me do as I like. This must mean they're the love of my life and I need to give them a relationship.* That shizzle doesn't make sense.

We humans are always grieving because we're constantly letting go of something even when we don't realize it. To evolve and grow, it means we have to let go of some things to gain some things. We experience the growth of grief.

People pleasing blocked us from grieving in a healthy way because it didn't allow us to feel, and so we couldn't process. Rather than it being a relatively clean pain, it became a dirty pain because of all the avoidance and self-harm that resulted.

If we keep saving up the expression of our feelings, the expression of ourselves, for emergency situations, to use against people when we want to cash in the debt of people pleasing, these feelings will catch us and others off guard, and they will always be unboundaried in those instances even if our actual *no*s or our concerns about issues are valid.

Loneliness is what we experience when we stop expressing our innermost feelings and thoughts to loved ones as well as ourselves. We feel emotionally adrift and cut off even though we might be surrounded by people. Expressing ourselves plugs us back into connection, and so we continue reclaiming our *no*s so that we say yes to life.

When we allow ourselves to consistently feel our feelings and recognize, acknowledge, and express them in our *yes*es, *no*s, and *maybe*s, we will not only evolve our communication and feel more secure in saying no, but we won't have to feel blindsided or taken hostage by our feelings. We won't feel cut off and alone. We'll also be able to trust our *yes*es and learn from those times when it becomes clear, with the benefit of hindsight, that we needed to say no.

By being more authentic with our *yes*es, grieving and processing our emotional baggage becomes part of the fabric of our day-to-day rather than thinking that we have to fix or prove ourselves before we can say no or being afraid of what life's challenges might reveal about us. We feel more resilient because we're not waiting for shit to pop off to finally pay attention to ourselves.

Professor Life will give pop quizzes. You will people-please on occasion and recognize it with the benefit of hindsight. This is okay. You will learn from it. Acknowledge what you were anxious about at the time so that you can use this data to help you make better decisions. Believe me, you will have the opportunity to say no again, so you don't need to sweat the *no* that you think got away from you! Go back through the steps. Pick one as your go-to, and you will gradually do the rest as a natural extension of it.

People pleasing is a habit that's been with you most or all of your life, so it's connected to your younger selves and your old identity. By approaching your *no* and boundaries with compassion, you will not be dismissive of yourself, including all your younger selves, and will recognize that you've traveled a journey to this point. The eruptions will dissipate and become few and far between. Challenges will become signals, opportunities, for you to level up your boundaries. The challenges will piss you off. Sometimes you'll be like, *What the hell does life want from me now? Didn't I already learn this?* And then you'll gradually figure it out.

Life presents you with people and situations to help you say no so that you can say yes to a more peaceful, enjoyable, authentic, joyful life.

People are going to feel what they're going to feel, think what they're going think, and do what they're going to do, no matter how "good" you are or how much you attempt to spare them from feeling discomfort, so you might as well get on with the business of being you from a place of love, care, trust, and respect for yourself *as well as* for others.

I'm Natalie Lue, and I'm a recovering people pleaser and I'm also happier and more me than I've ever been.

"Being you" means being everything you would be and do if you weren't so busy trying to please everyone else and *should*ing yourself. When you give yourself permission to show up more authentically, you become open to letting others do that too and helping break the cycle of shame and compliance. Go and be more you. Let yourself find the joy in saying no so that you become far more than you ever imagined.

ACKNOWLEDGMENTS

Jaysus, of all the chapters, I thought this one would be a doddle to write! Instead, the recovering people pleaser in me is like, *You'd better not leave anyone out!* Of course, I'm writing this from a place of desire, not obligation, so here goes.

For more than eighteen years, I've been blessed with the opportunity to share my stories and ideas online with a loving and generous audience around the world. Thank you, "Reclaimers," for giving me a career; for supporting my self-publishing journey and buying my books; and for trusting me with your stories and allowing me to help you to help yourselves to heal, grow, and learn.

The publishing industry is tough. I made a decision a long time ago to *choose myself* and not wait for someone to give me permission to share my work or be unabashedly myself. And thank feck I did because I was seventeen years into my writing journey by the time I got the deal for this book in March 2021! Of course, everything in its time.

I've experienced some painful knocks, and I remember, in autumn 2018, reaching this clear resolution that *I'm good.* If the traditional publishing journey was for me, I wasn't going to seek it out. I was also clear about what I needed if a book deal were to happen. And in July 2020, I got it.

Thank you to my super agents, Jan Baumer and Steve Troha at Folio Literary Management. You are exactly what I needed and wanted, and it's a joy to work with people who not only "get" me but who unequivocally have my back, love a good side-eye, and always make me belly laugh.

Thanks to Melissa and the rest of the foreign rights team, and shout-out to Anna Goldfarb for interviewing me for the *New York Times* piece that caught Folio's attention.

Thank you to the peeps at Harper Horizon and HarperCollins. Andrea Fleck-Nisbet and Amanda Bauch, I loved working together and so appreciate you investing in me. You were both so passionate about the book, and your feedback also helped me grow as a writer. Thank you, also, to Matt Baugher, Meaghan Porter, Kara Brammer, Kevin Smith, John Andrade, and Jeff Farr for bringing the book to life and your marketing and PR efforts. Belinda Bass and Grace Cavalier, thank you for working so hard to get to the right cover. I'm delighted with it! Themi Kartapanis in the UK, you're a sweetheart, and thanks for being a fountain of knowledge and great connector.

A big part of this phase of my creative journey is learning to ask for more help, so thanks, Josephine Brooks, for your online business management and everything you've done to prep for the launch of the book. I know it's required the patience of a saint at times, haha! Joanna Gorry, thanks for being a fab virtual assistant.

Rachel Coffey and Nikki Mellors, you were the first people to read my blog and didn't think twice about encouraging me. Rachel (and Sarah Grennan and Siobhan Cowler), thanks for the regular check-ups during the book-writing process. Thanks, Nikki, for always being the first person to read my books and your honest feedback.

Cate Sevilla, my belly-laughing homie (we sometimes laugh together so hard, we think we're going to throw up), thank you for hand-holding me through the entire book-writing process. Your advice and support have been invaluable.

Karen Arthur, my G, my dancing partner, and dirty-laughing famalam, thanks for all the chats and for being your brilliant self.

Susanna Reid, you are a gem, and thank you for your steadfast support over the years, nudging me to try the traditional publishing route, and our deep conversations.

Claire Archbold, I so appreciate all the work we've done together over the years and you telling it like it is. Gangster!

Kat Molesworth, the oracle, sage, and fellow lover of Nene Leakes gifs, thank you. I don't think you get enough recognition for how brilliant you are at being genuinely inclusive. Stay fabulous, and keep "making trouble."

Emma Gannon, thanks for the chats and giggles over dinner and for championing my work. It's so great to have someone to geek out with.

Thank you to the London Writers' Salon community for your support. What an amazing group! Matt and Parul, thank you for giving me so many shout-outs and for helping me take pride in my creative journey.

Big up to Caitlin Schiller, Sally Page, and the rest of the Blinkist crew. Your passion for *The Baggage Reclaim Sessions* is such a boost.

Thank you, also, to Natalie Gumede, Tabara N'Diaye, Jessica Huie, Ciara Shah, Luisa Omielan, Laura Hansen, Jessica Lauren, Rachael Lucas, Karen Cowell, Mima Lombardi, Tiffany Han, Nova Reid, Jenny Kakoudakis, Imriel Morgan, Salma Shah, Janet Murray, Helen Perry, Jolene Park, Tamu Thomas, Harriet Minter, Jenni Johnson, Jacqueline Colley, Sareta Fontaine, and Uju Asika.

To Sonia Desiderio, I'm so grateful I decided to "do" kinesiology. You set the ball rolling. Thank you for always telling it like it is and helping to heal my body from the built-up stress and trauma.

To my mentor and acupuncturist, Silvio Andrade, I never imagined I'd be writing this and you wouldn't be around to celebrate the book. Man, I miss you. Thank you for letting me cry on you so many times, it was hilarious, and for all your sage advice and wry comments that I hold close to my heart and do my best to embody every day.

Jassmine James, Fiona Dilston, and Mun Mah-Wing, thanks for helping me tune into myself and to learn the power of surrendering.

Beata Kallai-Kelbert, thanks for the weekly deep-tissue massages throughout the book-writing process and the wonderful chats.

Thank you to my big, bonkers family. Without the Lues, Cohens, Lauders, McCleans, and all my ancestors, I wouldn't be here, and I wouldn't be me.

To Mom "Mama" Pam, and my late father, Rupert, thank you for everything. Our relationships have been complex and bumpy but not without love. I see and hear you both. In particular, Mom, I appreciate every sacrifice you made to ensure we had a better life than you. Even though you were intensely about being academic and producing results, conversely, you are the person who gave me a love of all things creative. You are a badass. Dad, wherever you are, I know you're proud of me . . . and that your inner people pleaser's probably having a panic attack about this book ruffling the family's feathers. It'll be grand! Rest easy!

As my mischievous husband drunkenly pointed out in his wedding speech, "I'd like to thank Natalie's parents . . . all of them!," to howls of laughter from our guests, I have more than two parents. To my stepfather, Mike, thank you for being there and supporting pretty much anything I showed an interest in and planting the seeds to see self-employment as an opportunity instead of something to fear. To my stepmom, Jen, thanks for the love and for giving me my badass sisters. And thanks, Sylvia (stepfather's now-wife), for being your lovely self.

Thank you, also, to my in-laws, Emma and John, as well my mother-in-law's late husband "Uncle." Even though you're not quite sure what I do for work, I know I have your support.

Ireland, I love you and thank you. Even though it wasn't easy growing up as one of not-that-many black kids in the eighties and nineties, you loved me right back and have had a profound influence on me. Big shout-outs to the Corbawn and Shankill massive, the Cowlers, the Shankill O'Briens, Ballsbridge O'Briens, the Coffeys, Gilsenans, Bonasses, Carvossos, Normans, Cussens, Bradys, Levins, Crowells, Jacksons, and Carrolls. Thank you to my favorite headmistress, Mrs. Carroll at Our Lady of Good Counsel, the peeps at Loreto Dalkey, and Tiggy of Tiggy's Art School.

Roll-call time: Cathy, Tara, Ciara "Beaver," Fiona, Grace, Irene, Pamela, Michelle, Nac and the rest of the Mellors, Brenda and the Cuby gang, Gigi, Kim, Carys and the clan, Claire, Sadie and Bella, Beth and co., Bianca, Matt and the gang, Marilyn, Anne-Marie, Dina, Victoria, Amanda, Maryam, Kalisa and Patricia, Kareem and Maheni, Venessa and

Ollie, Jules and Hannah, David, Lorna, Becks, Eddie, Luciana "Lulu," Dino, Becky, Natasha, Anthony, Denis, and Philip, love you all.

Shout-out, also, to the Lue Girls' Book Club—aunty Sandra, Holly, and Sam.

Richard "Richie Rich," partners in crime since '79, thank you. We've been through a lot, and I'm so glad we've had each other. And sorry for outing your real age just there, haha. Sean, Martin, Sam, and Marie, love you. We're blessed to have one another.

Big up to my fab brother-in-laws, John, Ashley, and Elliot.

To my nieces and nephews, Kiah, Roman, Ace, Alex, Rishon, Lauryn, Ruibi, Lloyd, Keiko, Florence, and Albie, thanks for being your bright, hilarious selves.

To my dog, Chester Alvin King Jaffe Joffer, I couldn't leave you out as nobody puts Baby in the corner. Big love, my little stalker.

To my daughters, Saria and Nia, I'm always in awe of you and am honored to be your mother. Thank you for bearing with me during this book-writing process. Love you.

And, to my husband and bestie, Emmon, from the outset of our relationship, you've been unwaveringly supportive, never doubting my vision or ambition. Because you are unapologetically yourself, you've given me permission to bloom. You are a joy, and I love you.

NOTES

CHAPTER 2

1. Etymologeek, s.v. https://etymologeek.com/eng/good/40896046; Online Etymology Dictionary, s.v. "good (adj.)," https://www.etymonline.com/word/good.
2. Mayo Clinic Staff, "Chronic Stress Puts Your Health at Risk," Mayo Clinic, July 8, 2021, https://www.mayoclinic.org/healthy-lifestyle/stress-management/in -depth/stress/art-20046037.
3. Felix Richter, "The Great Resignation Record: How Many Americans Left Their Jobs in November 2021?" World Economic Forum, January 18, 2022, https:// www.weforum.org/agenda/2022/01/the-great-resignation-in-numbers -record/; Rashida Kamal, "Quitting Is Just Half the Story: The Truth Behind the 'Great Resignation,'" *The Guardian*, January 4, 2022, https://www.theguardian .com/business/2022/jan/04/great-resignation-quitting-us-unemployment -economy.
4. Nadine Burke Harris, MD, *The Deepest Well: Healing the Long-Term Effects of Childhood Trauma and Adversity* (London: Bluebird, 2018).
5. "Take the ACE Quiz—And Learn What It Does and Doesn't Mean," Center on the Developing Child, Harvard University, March 2, 2015, https://developingchild .harvard.edu/media-coverage/take-the-ace-quiz-and-learn-what-it-does-and -doesnt-mean/.
6. Jainish Patel and Prittesh Patel, "Consequences of Repression of Emotion: Physical Health, Mental Health and General Well Being," *International Journal of Psychotherapy Practice and Research* 1, no. 3 (2019): 16–21, https://openaccesspub.org /ijpr/article/999; Margaret Cullen, "How to Regulate Your Emotions Without Suppressing Them," *Greater Good Magazine*, January 30, 2020, https://greatergood .berkeley.edu/article/item/how_to_regulate_your_emotions_without_suppressing _them.

CHAPTER 5

1. Harris, *The Deepest Well*; Vincent J. Filetti et al., "Relationship of Childhood Abuse and Household Dysfunction to Many of the Leading Causes of Death in Adults: The Adverse Childhood Experiences (ACE) Study," *American Journal of Preven-*

tative Medicine 14, no. 4 (May 1, 1998), https://www.ajpmonline.org/article
/S0749-3797(98)00017-8/fulltext.

CHAPTER 6

1. Mélissa Godin, "Voluntourism: New Book Explores How Volunteer Trips Harm
    Rather Than Help," *The Guardian*, June 10, 2021, https://www.theguardian.com
    /global-development/2021/jun/10/voluntourism-new-book-explores-how
    -volunteer-trips-harm-rather-than-help; Eric Hartman, "Why UNICEF and
    Save the Children Are Against Your Short-Term Service in Orphanages," *Global
    SL Blog*, Campus Compact, September 5, 2014, https://compact.org/why-unicef
    -and-save-the-children-are-against-you-caring-for-orphans/; Ranjan Bandyopa-
    dhyay, "Volunteer Tourism and 'The White Man's Burden': Globalization of Suf-
    fering, White Savior Complex, Religion and Modernity," *Journal of Sustainable
    Tourism* 27, no. 3 (2019): 327–43, https://www.tandfonline.com/doi/abs/10.1080
    /09669582.2019.1578361?.

CHAPTER 10

1. Ariana Orvell, et al., "Does Distanced Self-Talk Facilitate Emotion Regulation
    Across a Range of Emotionally Intense Experiences?" *Clinical Psychological Science*
    9, no. 1 (January 2021): 68–78, https://journals.sagepub.com/doi/abs/10.1177
    /2167702620951539.

CHAPTER 13

1. Gabby Bernstein, "How to Use the Abraham-Hicks Emotional Guidance Scale,"
    GabbyBernstein.com, February 2, 2020, https://gabbybernstein.com/emotional
    -guidance-scale-abraham-hicks/.

INDEX